# The Making of Modern Africa

**Series Editors:** Abebe Zegeye and John Higginson

*Environment, Health and Population Displacement*
Andrew E. Collins

*International Banking and Rural Development*
Pade Badru

*Structural Adjustment and Mass Poverty in Ghana*
Kwabena Donkor

*Contemporary Issues in Socio-economic Reform in Zambia*
Edited by Herrick C. Mpuku and Ivan Zyuulu

*The State and Organised Labour in Botswana*
Monageng Mogalakwe

*Small African Towns - between Rural Networks
and Urban Hierarchies*
Poul Ove Pedersen

*Regional Cooperation and Integration within Industry
and Trade in Southern Africa*
Jens Haarlov

*From Self-Help Housing to Sustainable Settlement*
John Tait

*Ominous Transition*
Joye Bowman

*Contemporary Issues in Regional Development Policy*
Edited by Wilbert Gooneratne and Robert Obudho

*Religious Militancy and Self-Assertion*
Toyin Falola and Matthew Hassan Kukah

# GROWTH OR STAGNATION?
# SOUTH AFRICA HEADING FOR THE YEAR 2000

# Growth or Stagnation? South Africa heading for the year 2000

MATS LUNDAHL
*Stockholm School of Economics*

Routledge
Taylor & Francis Group

LONDON AND NEW YORK

First published 1999 by Ashgate Publishing

Reissued 2018 by Routledge
2 Park Square, Milton Park, Abingdon, Oxon, OX14 4RN
52 Vanderbilt Avenue, New York, NY 10017

*Routledge is an imprint of the Taylor & Francis Group, an informa business*

Notice:
Product or corporate names may be trademarks or registered trademarks, and are used only for identification and explanation without intent to infringe.

Publisher's Note
The publisher has gone to great lengths to ensure the quality of this reprint but points out that some imperfections in the original copies may be apparent.

Disclaimer
The publisher has made every effort to trace copyright holders and welcomes correspondence from those they have been unable to contact.

A Library of Congress record exists under LC control number:

ISBN 13: 978-0-367-02489-5 (hbk)
ISBN 13: 978-0-429-39925-1 (ebk)

# Contents

| | | |
|---|---|---|
| *Acknowledgements* | | vi |
| *Preface* | | vii |
| 1 | Political success and economic distress: South Africa at the threshold of the twenty-first century | 1 |
| 2 | The South African economy after apartheid | 19 |
| 3 | The economy of transition: South Africa at the turn of the century | 31 |
| 4 | The post-apartheid economy, and after? | 45 |
| 5 | The South African economy in 1996: From Reconstruction and Development to Growth, Employment and Redistribution | 73 |
| 6 | The new South Africa: growth or stagnation? | 123 |
| *Index* | | 147 |

# Acknowledgements

Most of the essays contained in the present volume have been published as journal articles or book chapters. They are reprinted with the kind permission of the publishers. The provenance of the chapters is as follows:

*Chapter 2*: Internationella Studier 1, 1995, pp. 40-52 (translated from the Swedish). Reprinted with permission from Internationella Studier, the Swedish Institute of International Affairs, Stockholm.

*Chapter 3*: Lars Jonung (ed.), Ekonomisk politik i omvandling. The Economic Research Institute, Stockholm School of Economics, Stockholm 1995, pp. 148-158 (translated from the Swedish). Reprinted with permission from the Economic Research Institute, Stockholm School of Economics, Stockholm.

*Chapter 4*: Lennart Petersson (ed.), Post-Apartheid Southern Africa: Economic challenges and policies for the future. London and New York: Routledge, 1998, pp. 21-43. Reprinted with permission from Routledge, London and New York.

*Chapter 5*: The South African Economy in 1996: From Reconstruction and Development to Growth, Employment and Redistribution. Macroeconomic Report, 1997:3, SIDA, Stockholm. Reprinted with permission from the Swedish International Development Cooperation Agency, Stockholm.

*Chapter 6*: Steve Kayizzi-Mugerwa (ed.), The African Economy: Policy, institutions and the future. London and New York: Routledge, 1999, pp. 213-232. Reprinted with permission from Routledge, London and New York.

# Preface

The essays collected in the present volume derive from an interest in South Africa and its economy which goes back to the early 1970s, when I wrote my first piece on the economics of discrimination. This later resulted in a book on that subject, with applications fetched from South Africa, as well as in a number of journal articles, later collected in book form. The second chapter of my South African story began in 1990 with the writing of a series of macroeconomic reports for the Swedish International Development Authority (SIDA), most of them together with Lena Moritz. This effort culminated in a book in Swedish, published in 1996.

The present pieces have all been written between 1994 and 1999. With the exception of the first, and most recent, chapter, they are presented here in the chronological writing order. The idea is that, to some extent, this should make it possible to follow how the debate on the South African economy has evolved since the fall of the apartheid regime.

Chapters 2 and 3 have been written together with Lena Moritz - the latest products in a very fruitful and pleasant cooperation, but hopefully not the last ones. Lena has given her kind permission to let me reproduce them here. With a minimum of time at his disposal, Michael Pretes has checked the English of the newly written chapter and the chapters translated from the Swedish. Carin Blomkvist has prepared both the index and the camera-ready manuscript, after an incredibly short learning period, and besides, in her usual cheerful manner, spotted a number of inaccuracies in the references. To all three I extend my gratitude.

*Stockholm, February 1999*
*Mats Lundahl*

# 1 Political success and economic distress: South Africa at the threshold of the twenty-first century

As South Africa approaches the next millennium, the country's main problem is how to rid itself of the consequences of a legacy that has plagued it for almost 350 years: the legacy of race discrimination. Ever since their first arrival in southern Africa, the Europeans made it clear that the development they had in mind was one that paid little attention to the peoples who were there before them. As the subsequent history of South Africa amply demonstrates, the creation of an explicit apartheid ideology following the triumph of the National Party in the 1948 parliamentary elections was nothing but the culmination of a process that had begun centuries before.

With the passage of time, however, the apartheid system would become an anachronism – increasingly out of touch with economic and social reality. Pressure would arise both inside South Africa and outside, on the international scene, to reform and eliminate it. This pressure existed even inside the National Party. Towards the end of the 1970s it was an open question whether the party would opt for reforms and, if so, to what extent.

It would take another decade before the decisive change took place. P.W. Botha had to leave and F.W. de Klerk take over before the road to democracy, majority rule, and equality between the races could be tread. At the beginning of the 1990s, however, the reform process gathered a strong momentum. The political scene underwent a complete change in a handful of years. Democratic elections were held in 1994, a Government of National Unity took over, and a new constitution was forged. Politically, the 'new' South Africa has been a success. Negotiation and consensus solutions have driven confrontation out of the arena.

The economic picture, however, is entirely different. The number one demand on the new government has been to redress the racial inequalities that had accumulated for over three centuries, and especially those that were results of the Nationalist policy. This has proved to be a much more difficult process than that of laying the foundations for political democracy. In the wake of apartheid, South Africa emerged with a highly distorted economy in dire need of reforms, an economy which furthermore offered little scope for short-run redistribution. There are, however, no panaceas when it comes to growth, and the results so far have been disappointing. The rate of change of GDP has barely been high enough to outstrip population growth during the past several years and no change appears to be in sight.

The economic program of the Government of National Unity proved to contain major inconsistencies between the delivery of basic needs, the public investment needed to meet these goals and the economic growth rate. Accordingly, a new macroeconomic strategy had to be launched – one that makes growth paramount, but simultaneously one that runs the risk of foundering on the rock of insufficient investment incentives. The immediate future does not look very bright, especially considering recent international economic events. The Asian crisis could portend a period of slowed international growth, with negative consequences for South Africa as well.

## Origins of a racially segregated society[1]

During the first phase of white domination, which extended from the arrival of the Dutch in 1652 to the mineral discoveries in the late nineteenth century, a European, agriculture-based economy emerged, and it was mainly in the land market that discrimination took place. The Europeans gradually moved the frontier northwards from the Cape, depriving the Africans of their land in the process. Land alienation also helped contribute to the creation of a worker class that could be brought to serve the Europeans.[2]

As the structure of the economy changed in the wake of substantial mineral discoveries, notably gold, so did the character of discrimination. The main issue no longer was land, but rather labor. Towards the end of the nineteenth century, African farmers emerged as successful competitors to the Europeans in the produce markets. This ran counter to the interests of the latter. Miners and farmers both needed workers, at the lowest possible wage. An alliance was forged between gold and maize, backed by government-enforced monopsonistic recruitment of workers for the mines.

The low-wage policy, however, hurt European workers. Towards the end of the nineteenth century an exodus of whites began from the South African countryside. The combination of small farm size, obsolete methods, new demands following the increasing commercialization of agriculture, and outright physical damage caused by the Boer War, forced one out of eight to leave rural areas and migrate to urban districts in search of a job. There, however, they had to face the competition of Africans who undercut them in wage terms, very much as a result of the white labor market policies.

After a violent clash between government troops and white workers on the Witwatersrand in 1922, workers used their franchise two years later to vote the Jan Smuts government out and the so-called Pact Government – an alliance between farmers and workers – in. This was the beginning of a more elaborate set of laws and rules reserving jobs for whites in the labor market. From the mid-1920s a formal color bar was erected that not only reserved the best jobs for whites but also instituted a 'civilized labor policy' giving whites precedence when competing with Africans for unskilled work.

Tensions were thus built into the labor market. Paying higher wages to workers, white or black, was hardly in the interest of capital owners in mining and industry. On the contrary, over the next decades they would oppose government interference in employment and wage matters. Time increasingly was to prove them right. The importance of manufacturing in the South African economy grew and at the same time mining technology was becoming more sophisticated. Gradually, the demand for labor shifted from the unskilled towards more educated workers, but the color bar did not facilitate this change.

Developments in the political arena did not pave the way for economic change either. In 1948, the National Party won the parliamentary elections and immediately set out to create a society based on systematic race discrimination.[3] The cornerstone of this policy was *apartheid*, or separation of the races. The Nationalists proceeded to alter the electoral system to advance their interests to eliminate the limited franchise of other racial groups, and to regulate all aspects of South African social and economic life through an incredibly detailed and Byzantine body of laws. By the mid-1960s, virtually all the important building blocks of this policy were in place.

The right of Africans to acquire land in South Africa had been severely circumscribed by legislation in 1913 and 1936. The Nationalists continued this policy, carrying it to its extreme. Beginning in 1951, the 13.8 percent of the territory that had been reserved for Africans were split into first eight

3

and later ten 'homelands' that often consisted of non-contiguous areas. There, and nowhere else, was where the Africans 'belonged', according to Hendrik Verwoerd, then Minister of Native Affairs. Only those Africans who possessed special permits were allowed to enter 'white' areas, and then only as workers. The rest were ordered out, with or without explicit assistance from the police. Twenty-five years later, the first of these homelands, the Transkei, was declared 'independent' by the Nationalist government, to be followed by three more over the next five years.

White capital owners were not the only group to oppose the codification and tightening of racial discrimination. The victims reacted as well. The African National Congress (ANC), founded in 1912, the Pan-Africanist Congress (PAC), dating from 1959, and other, similar bodies organized protests until, in 1960, both the ANC and the PAC were outlawed through a specially written Unlawful Organizations Act. Subsequently those of their leaders who did not manage to go into exile were put on trial and jailed. From the mid-1960s both the ANC and the PAC were seriously weakened. At this point, both of them had also drawn the conclusion that peaceful resistance was useless and founded military wings. The relations between the government and the governed had entered a stalemate phase.

During this phase, resistance began to seek new forms. One of these was represented by Inkatha, which had been founded in 1928 as a Zulu cultural movement. From 1975, however, under the leadership of Mangosuthu Buthelezi, the nominal administrator of the KwaZulu homeland, Inkatha was turned into a political organization. At first, the new movement worked closely with the ANC, but in 1978 the two organizations clashed, and henceforth Inkatha stood out as a limited, ethnically-based grouping. Another, broader, strand of resistance was represented by organizations based on the concept of Black Consciousness, organizations which in principle did not cooperate with Europeans. These movements quickly ran into trouble, however, and their leaders were jailed, exiled or killed by the police, like Steve Biko in 1977.

International resistance to South African racial policies was building up during the postwar period. Such incidents as the killing and wounding of unarmed demonstrators in Sharpeville in 1960 and of school children in Soweto in 1976 alerted the international community about the brutality of the system, and trade and investment sanctions of varying scope and intensity were imposed. These sanctions, however, did not have much impact. With assistance of countries such as Rhodesia and Iran, South Africa was able to circumvent the sanctions. Apartheid reigned supreme.

## The turning tide

Things would soon start to change. The 1970s were a worrisome decade in South Africa. It became clear that the apartheid system could not survive for ever. Some observers argued that in the short and medium term the apartheid regime was stable,[4] among other things because the Western powers would not apply any pressure. According to this view, South Africa was too important for the West both in military and economic terms to be handed over to a majority government with uncertain intentions.

This stability prediction would turn out to be wrong, but not because of external pressure. The apartheid system had played an essential role in the build-up of the growth machinery that fueled the South African economy from the time of the mineral discoveries in the late nineteenth century until the beginning of the 1970s. But with the passage of time the system became a dysfunctional anachronism that retarded economic progress. Instead of oiling the economy, apartheid slowed it down.[5]

During the administration of P.W. Botha it was already apparent that a choice was imminent for the National Party. When the party won the 1948 elections its constituency had been relatively homogeneous: a majority of Afrikaner farmers and workers. Both these groups had been stern defenders of apartheid, the workers because racial discrimination protected them from competition in the labor market, and the farmers because excluding Africans from urban jobs served to keep the agricultural wage down. Over the course of the next three decades this state of affairs was to change. The structure of the Afrikaner community in 1978 was not the same as in 1948. What had happened in the meantime was that a class of Afrikaner capitalists had been created. Whereas in 1948 the Afrikaners had owned less than 10 percent of the non-agricultural private sector, thirty years later the figure had increased to 25 percent.[6] In addition, they were not mainly blue-collar workers any longer. In 1975 the percentage of Afrikaners in white-collar occupations had risen to 65, to be compared with 28 in 1948.[7]

The shift in the socioeconomic composition of Afrikaner society was reflected in the policies of the National Party. The 'new' Afrikaner groups did not share the traditional views of apartheid. As capitalists they had acquired an interest in efficiency and competition among workers. As white-collar, as opposed to blue-collar, workers they were interested in preserving the color bar in education, but not policies that made it difficult to recruit Africans to urban blue-collar jobs.

5

In 1978, when P.W. Botha succeeded John Vorster as party leader,[8] he instituted a halfhearted change in policy. The Botha period was characterized by jerky movements in different directions. Since the late 1960s the National Party had been weakened by the conflicts between *verligtes* and *verkramptes*, i.e. between those who wanted to reform the apartheid system and those who stuck to it more or less in the form it had been given by Verwoerd. In this situation, Botha, himself a *verligte*, had to strike a balance that would not create splinter groups either on the right or on the left.

This was not an easy task. In principle compromises were impossible, so Botha opted for a course where satisfaction would alternate between the two groups. This type of compensation policy failed, however. Botha was convinced that economic growth could only result from more liberal policies, but this tended to produce defection among the conservative elements in his party who hence had to be soothed by promises of law and order and continued white control. As time went by, the situation grew increasingly impossible. In the 1981 parliamentary elections, the Nationalists obtained almost 80 percent of the seats. Botha interpreted this as a mandate for his *verligte* line and attempted to force the conservative opposition within the party, led by Andries Treurnicht, into the background. The attempt failed, however, and the following year Treurnicht and his group left the Nationalist fold to form their own Conservative Party. It had proved impossible to satisfy both factions.

What followed was a series of pseudo-reforms. Botha shared the conviction that the whites were to continue to rule South Africa. In 1984, a constitutional 'solution' was presented in the form of a tricameral parliament, with a strong white majority, where Coloreds and Asians were to 'share' power with the whites. The Africans were not invited to participate, and the apartheid system as such underwent only minor changes. As a result of the work of two government commissions, African trade unions were allowed, the rules governing the geographical mobility of labor were changed, and towards the end of the 1980s the deportations of Africans who lacked permits to enter areas designed as whites ceased. A number of 'petty apartheid' laws were abolished.

These steps were very marginal. Botha did not stay in power long enough to have to make the crucial decision of whether to tighten apartheid again or to go for a more profound reform strategy. Illness hit him, in the form of a stroke in January 1989, and, much against his will, Botha left the presidency in August the same year.

## The road to 1994[9]

The turning point came with the appointment of F.W. de Klerk as party leader and president. In the 1989 elections the Nationalists obtained a mere 48 percent of the votes, against 57 percent in 1981. It was obvious that Botha's attempt to woo both the traditional support groups and the 'new' Afrikaners had failed. The party lost 27 seats in Parliament, both to the Conservative Party on the right and the Democratic Party on the left.[10] The new leader was forced to make a critical choice.

Nothing in de Klerk's solidly conservative background prepared the South Africans for what was going to come. After seventeen years in Parliament, having held six different portfolios, he had not been behind a single reform proposal. His opening speech to Parliament, in February 1990, consequently came as a complete surprise. In this, he announced the lifting of the ban on the ANC, the PAC and the Communist Party, the unconditional release of Nelson Mandela, and the scrapping of a number of restrictions on the activities of the mass media, trade unions and political parties. The new president also stressed the importance of future negotiations between all groups in South African society in order to create a society where all citizens had equal rights.[11]

The 'Rubicon' speech delivered by de Klerk did not, however, mean that the road to a democratic, egalitarian society with majority rule would be a smooth one. One by one the apartheid laws were scrapped, but the president was quite adamant about his views of African majority rule. In post-apartheid South Africa there had to be strong guarantees of minority rights and a division of power, and the National Party put forward a proposal establishing a bicameral parliament to this end.

This proposal was unacceptable to the ANC, however, and a period of complicated, time-consuming, and frustrating negotiations against a backdrop of periodic violence ensued, which would not end until the democratic elections at the end of April 1994. Naturally, the protagonists in this process were de Klerk and Mandela, but they were far from the only ones involved. On the contrary, the negotiations were opened to all the political actors on the South African scene and these could only act with a minimum approval of their respective constituencies. In other words, the ride ahead would be a bumpy one, given the highly diverging interests of the ANC, the National Party, Inkatha, the Conservatives, the Democratic Party, and the splinter groups on the African left and the white right.

7

Despite innumerable obstacles it proved possible to bring the negotiation process to a happy end, against all odds. As Timothy Sisk has pointed out, South Africa has been one of the most deeply divided societies in the world during the present century,[12] one which to a large extent has been driven by identity politics based on race and other ethnic characteristics. To overcome the deep divisions between the various interest groups, create 'sufficient consensus' of opinion, prepare democratic elections, establish a Government of National Unity and institute majority rule has been no small feat.

A number of steps were required before the process converged. When de Klerk delivered his inaugural speech the old system had just begun to crumble. The economic contradictions of apartheid in combination with the pressure from the international community was making it difficult to sustain it, and de Klerk realized that the end would have to come sooner or later. The Nationalists could not continue to muddle through forever. One way or the other they would have to relinquish power or at least share it. Their problem was to find the best way of doing so.

In the past, the Nationalist view of politics in South Africa, and racial politics in particular, had been of a largely zero-sum kind. The African majority, if given the power to act politically and vote, would not concede any role to the National Party. Their gains would be the Nationalists' loss. Similarly, the ANC – through decades of painful experience – had learnt that Afrikaner Nationalists thought of government as white supremacy. Its negotiators had good reasons for fearing that little would come out of the political process ahead.

These attitudes changed, however, during the course of the negotiation process. The situation threatened to degenerate into a Prisoners' Dilemma, with the two protagonists painting themselves into their respective corners, stubbornly opting for strategies based on mistrust and power demonstrations that would have left them far worse off than cooperative strategies based on negotiations and concessions. Gradually, however, it dawned on both the ANC and the National Party that a unilateral solution would be impossible. No party could dictate the outcome of the negotiations to the other, and a refusal to make concessions would simply make things worse in the future. Stonewalling would produce political stalemate and economic stagnation. The perception of the nature of the negotiations thus changed from a zero-sum game to a positive-sum one.

Nevertheless the negotiations took time. The period from de Klerk's 'Rubicon' speech to the National Peace Accord in September 1991 has been characterized by Timothy Sisk as a preliminary phase, where the emphasis was on 'talks about talks'.[13] During this phase, formal constitutional negotiations were prepared and the rules and conditions for them were laid down. Arriving at these rules was not easy. The 'old' suspicions crept back into the picture from time to time. Demands were phrased in ultimate terms and escalating violence threatened the outcome all the way to the end; clashes between ANC and Inkatha supporters and acts of terrorism from extreme white right-wingers took place. On a number of occasions the negotiations threatened to break down, but each time it proved possible to get back on track. The lesson was driven home that without continued negotiations nothing would be achieved.

In this way, it proved possible to overcome the potentially disastrous effects of the 'Inkathagate' scandal, when in July 1991 it was revealed that the Nationalist government had financed Inkatha mass rallies. Faced with this fact, de Klerk reacted by reshuffling his government, moving the most compromised ministers away from the portfolios of defense and law and order, respectively. The credibility of his government, however, had been severely shaken, and it was clear that the National Party was no longer in a position to control the process whereby a new South Africa was being shaped. The ANC now held the upper hand in the negotiations and the government had no other choice than proceeding towards its own eventual removal. In September, with dissatisfied Inkatha supporters rallying in the streets of Johannesburg, the National Peace Accord was signed by de Klerk, Mandela, Buthelezi, and representatives of 29 other organizations committing themselves to keeping peace, without, however, much enthusiasm on any part.

In particular, the constituencies of the signatories had not been convinced of the necessity to move ahead together, making concessions to the 'adversaries' as the negotiations went along. Moreover, extremists attempted to derail the negotiations, outbidding the parties involved in terms of promises and resorting to periodic violence. Nevertheless, at the end of 1991, a phase of more substantial negotiations about the transition to majority rule could begin.

This phase, which extended from late 1991 to late 1993, was as turbulent and confused as the 'preliminary' one. Economically, it was a period of stagnation and decline until a turning point was reached in May 1993. Politically, there was strong competition between parties, with continued violence on critical occasions. The start of this phase began in December 1991 with the first talks of the Convention for a Democratic South Africa (CODESA). The decision rule governing CODESA was that of 'sufficient consensus', i.e. agreement between the ANC and the government (and possibly other parties as well), which had been laid down in bilateral talks between the two main protagonists before the formal convention began. The first CODESA talks produced a Declaration of Intent, endorsed by seventeen signatories, on a non-racial state, multiparty democracy, universal suffrage, and proportional representation of parties in Parliament, and CODESA was set up as a standing institution.

In March 1992, after the Nationalists had been defeated by the Conservative Party in a by-election, de Klerk called a whites-only referendum on his reforms and negotiations with the ANC. He won a stunning 68.6 percent of the votes. This allowed him to go into the second round of CODESA, in May, with renewed self-confidence, having minimized the threat from his right. By the same token, however, it contributed to producing an impasse on the procedure for decision making with respect to the regions. CODESA II failed because for a moment both the ANC and the government took a step backwards, into their old beliefs that it would be possible to push the other party into an agreement.

In June, Inkatha supporters raided a workers' hostel in Boipatong, south of Johannesburg – an ANC stronghold – and left 49 dead. The ANC suspended further talks and the Congress of South African Trade Unions (COSATU) called a general strike at the beginning of August. The ANC then marched on Bisho, the capital of the 'independent' homeland of Ciskei, in order to overthrow the Nationalist-allied dictator there. The Ciskei forces opened fire, killing 28 and wounding around 200 people. This event had the effect of rallying the negotiators back to the table. The mutual feeling that the entire democratization process was threatened was held above desires to inflict further injury on political adversaries.

A Record of Understanding was signed on 26 September, and the parties agreed that an elected constituent assembly would also serve as an interim parliament, that this assembly would draft the new constitution, and that an interim Government of National Unity should be constituted under the umbrella of an interim constitution. The ANC agreed to cut down on mass action and to endorse a general amnesty, to be granted by the interim government. Inkatha, however, refused to sign, and there was a considerable split within the ranks of both the ANC and the government. Among the former dissatisfaction was voiced with the promise of amnesty, and among the latter some ministers favored cooperating with Inkatha instead of with the ANC.

Later, however, bilateral agreement would prevail. Only following such agreement would issues be brought to multilateral negotiations. The ANC quickly closed its ranks. Communist Party chairman Joe Slovo had realized that the ANC did not possess enough trained people to govern South Africa in the post-apartheid period. The vast majority of the existing Afrikaner bureaucrats would be needed and irritating this group could easily prompt the bureaucracy to sabotage reform efforts. In a document on negotiation presented to the ANC leadership he argued that, as a matter of strategic retreat, but not retreat in matters of principle, the ANC would do best if it favored an interim period of power-sharing before entering the final stage of majority rule. His argument proved irrefutable. After a stormy debate the ANC executive committee made it the official line. On the other side, de Klerk retired 23 military officers for having staged covert operations against the ANC.

With these two events, the stage was set for a Democratization Pact between the ANC and the Nationalist government. The negotiations had resulted in a breakthrough. The details of the pact still had to be negotiated, however. These negotiations took place at the beginning of 1993, when the two major groupings agreed to the drafting of an interim constitution, elections to a constituent assembly which was to draft and adopt a new constitution, an interim government based on the outcome of these elections, with representation for all parties with more than 5 percent of the votes, a two-thirds decision rule in the constituent assembly, and a five-year transition period before the adoption of majority rule in elections under the new constitution.

The Democratization Pact was thereafter presented to the other parties in a Multiparty Negotiating Process (MPNP), disturbed by events like the murder of Communist Party general secretary Chris Hani by a white extremist and a deranged commando attack by the Afrikaner Weerstands-beweging (AWB) on the Johannesburg World Trade Centre, where the negotiations were being held, as well as new violent clashes between ANC and Inkatha supporters, resulting in high death tolls. The pact could not be stopped, however. In November, the draft interim constitution was adopted in the MPNP, and the stage was set for the elections that were to take place on 27 April 1994. The Old (1948) Order had come to an end in South Africa.

## Politics and economics

The negotiation process that had begun in 1991 had produced a solution that managed to reconcile the requirement that majority rule be adopted with protection of the rights of the minorities through their representation in Parliament and government during the transition period. The major players in the political process had gained enough, or at least managed to avoid unacceptable losses to such an extent that they accepted the eventual outcome. One of the most divided societies in the world had managed to find a peaceful solution based on concessions and mutual gains. The political process that developed in South Africa between 1991 and 1994 was a success. It had proved possible to peacefully overcome innumerable obstacles on the road to general elections and democracy. The positive-sum perception had triumphed.

The essays in the present book deal not with politics but with the economic problems facing post-apartheid South Africa. Will the country be able to overcome its unpalatable legacy in this sphere as well? In one sense the characteristics of the economic problems resemble the political problems of 1991 through 1994, i.e. if groups fail to cooperate the outcome will be worse for all of them. South Africa continues to be characterized by social tensions of various kinds (and in the post-apartheid setting new tensions tend to arise as well). The most important single challenge facing South African society today is that of reducing the gaps in living standards between the white minority and the other population groups, notably the Africans. In the subsequent chapters of the book I argue that there is no easy way to do this. It is easy enough, however, to make the task an impossible one.

The business community, the trade unions and the government all possess the power to throw a wrench into the economic machinery. The debate of how to create an economy with the necessary power of redistribution has therefore to some extent revolved around the desirability of creating mechanisms whereby these three power centers can be made to cooperate in the process of economic policy making through making mutual concessions. Attempts have been made to institutionalize the cooperation, above all through the creation of the National Economic, Development and Labour Council (NEDLAC), a forum for consultations on issues related to economic growth, social equality, and participation in economic decision making.[14] Four groups are represented in NEDLAC. In addition to the business-unions-government triad, community and development organizations have been invited, but these carry less weight than the other three participants.

The idea is that NEDLAC should establish consensus solutions that resemble those forged in the political arena. Major questions relating to labor market legislation and changes of economic and social policy are to be dealt with in this way before decisions are made in Parliament. The key area here is the labor market, because it is precisely there that the business community is facing the labor unions directly and it is where their interests are likely to diverge most. As a result, a government commission on labor market policies has singled out this issue for special consideration and suggested that both employers and employees should be prepared to bring to the negotiation table a specific set of concessions which they can trade with each other and with the government (in return for specific services from the latter). If this works out, the thinking goes, signals are sent to prospective investors that the South African policy environment is a stable and reliable one and that money can be confidently and productively invested in the country.

Again, the idea is one of converting a possible zero-sum game with Prisoners' Dilemma overtones into a positive-sum game where mutual concessions make everybody better off. To what extent this is possible is, however, a different question. The analogy with the political process that put South Africa on the road to democracy is not necessarily valid.

For example, the extent to which NEDLAC has been successful is disputed. NEDLAC in 1995 sprang out of the National Economic Forum (NEC) that had been created in 1992, during a period of intense political negotiation. In both cases the idea was to create a decision-making process in the economic and social field that would be viewed as transparent and democratic. Admittedly, NEDLAC has helped in the construction of a new Labour Relations Act, but it is far from certain that the type of corporatist decision-making that NEDLAC represents will be able to work in the long run. Labor and business have a history of interests that differ widely from each other, and the historical differences of course continue to exist. Without government interference it would probably not have been possible to bring the two to the corporatist discussion and negotiation table. The representation of business, in particular, may be difficult, because decisions made in fora like NEDLAC may easily run counter to the logic of the market, and the constituency that the business negotiators represent will continue to act mainly through the market. It may even be that the government itself feels that NEDLAC-bargained solutions interfere with the ability of the government to make decisions.

However, the main difference between the political process and the economic one is that the latter unfolds in the market. This fact is of central importance when it comes to devising a credible strategy for economic development and redistribution in South Africa. The destruction of the economic legacy of apartheid cannot be achieved at the negotiation table – only in the market place. The role of private enterprise is a crucial one. Unless domestic and foreign investors can be convinced that South Africa is a country where their money will be both safe and productive, the wheels will not start rolling fast enough to make redistribution a reality.

Very few people would question the need for redistribution. Of all countries for which data are available it is South Africa that presents the most unequal distribution of income, and the differences follow ethnic lines. It hardly matters which economic or social indicator you choose. The outcome will be the same: a completely unacceptable gap between the white minority and the other ethnic groups. The problem is finding the best strategy for closing that gap. Various aspects of this problem are discussed in the remainder of this book.

Chapter 2, 'The South African economy after apartheid', gives a brief overview of the challenge of bringing the economy from a situation where the growth of GDP in real terms has barely been enough to outstrip the growth of the population, to one of sustained growth of a magnitude that allows the redistributive program contained in the Reconstruction and Development Programme (RDP) of the ANC to be carried out. It sketches developments in the economy until 1994, gives a short review of the main contents of the RDP and discusses some key issues of trade and industrial policy.

Chapter 3, 'The economy of transition: South Africa at the turn of the century', centers on the redistribution issue. It presents some of the basic statistics with respect to existing inequalities. Thereafter it goes on to discuss how much redistribution could take place within the limits set by the government budget, a mere 2–3 percent of the 1991/92 GDP. Given this, it is clear that no serious redistributive effort will succeed unless the economy grows. The RDP is formulated essentially as a basic needs program, but it also envisages a real growth rate of GDP of 5 percent per annum at the beginning of the twenty-first century.

Growth will not come automatically. If it materializes it may easily conflict with stabilization in the short run, notably Reserve Bank efforts to prevent a balance of payments deficit as growth results in an increased demand for imports. It could also be threatened by demands for wage increases. Nor is it clear just what is needed to start the growth process. One school of thought has advocated a sequence that starts with redistribution – in a way that boosts the domestic demand for labor-intensive goods, and hence employment and incomes as well. This scenario will not necessarily work, however, as the marginal propensity of low-income groups to consume may not be directed exclusively, or even mainly, towards labor-intensive goods. Thus, growth will have to be achieved through industrial exports, and South Africa has accordingly embarked on a gradual dismantling of the protective barriers that were built from the 1920s to the end of the apartheid era.

Chapter 4, 'The post-apartheid economy, and after?', opens with a sketch of the main 'achievements' of the apartheid system, not only in terms of inequality between the races but also from the perspective of inefficiency in the allocation of resources in the economy. The second section provides an account of how the economic goals of the ANC were shaped at the beginning of the 1990s, at a point when nothing beyond the vague and contradictory statements contained in the Freedom Charter was available to guide future action. The outcome was the Reconstruction and Development Programme.

Once the implementation of the RDP began, after the victory of the ANC in the April 1994 elections, it was soon discovered that making the program work was far from easy. The visions of the government were challenged both by the South African Foundation, one of the organizations speaking for business, and by the trade union movement, but from very different angles. This was perhaps to be expected. Far worse was the discovery that with current growth and investment rates the RDP stood no chance whatsoever of being implemented. A new macroeconomic growth strategy was required: the Growth, Employment and Redistribution (GEAR) program.

The contents of GEAR are analyzed in Chapter 4 and in Chapter 5, 'The South African economy in 1996: From Reconstruction and Development to Growth, Employment, and Redistribution'. The causality in GEAR runs from growth to employment and redistribution: without growth it will not be possible to close the economic gap between the four ethnic groups of South Africa. The actual growth rate of GDP since the turning point in May 1993 until the first quarter of 1996 was around 3 percent per annum on average. For the latter year as a whole the figure was slightly higher, 3.2 percent, whereas in 1997 a setback was registered, with growth falling back to a mere 1.7 percent, as agricultural production fell back to 'normal' levels from the 1996 record.[15] The figures revealed so far for 1998 are even worse: 0.5 percent on an annual basis for the first two quarters.[16] Possibly, a recovery will take place during the last six months,[17] but a weak performance in mining and manufacturing will no doubt contribute to an end of the year figure which is clearly below the 1995 (3.4 percent) and 1996 (3.2 percent) figures and possibly also below the 1.7 percent growth registered in 1997.[18]

Stimulating growth to the desired figure of over 6 percent in 2000 obviously calls for special efforts. Gross investment growth has declined persistently over the past three years, from 10.3 percent in 1995 to 7.8 in 1998 and 3.5 in 1997, but has picked up during the first two quarters of 1998, largely as a result of public spending on expanding telecommunications.[19] Public investment is, however, hardly the key to future growth. Private investment is, however, and according to GEAR this will be stimulated through a government policy stressing fiscal and monetary discipline and a trade and exchange rate policy that makes South Africa competitive in the international markets for manufactures.

Whether signals of a tight and responsible economic policy will make domestic and foreign investors increase their stakes in South Africa remains to be seen. They may also serve to dampen the growth rate. As analyzed in Chapter 4, Chapter 5 and in Chapter 6, 'The new South Africa: growth or stagnation?', investors may be more interested in expanding markets than in policy discipline, and discipline works mainly by restricting demand. Foreign investors, in particular, may want to make sure that South African companies view the future with confidence before they choose South Africa over alternative locations.

Given that discipline seems to be the key word, it is difficult to escape the conclusion that GEAR seems to be more of a stabilization strategy than a growth strategy. South Africa may have to enter the next millennium with a growth rate that is far below what was hoped for when the Reconstruction and Development Programme was drawn up. The transition years when the country was governed by a Government of National Unity may be recalled as a period of muddling through rather than the period when the obstacles to sustained growth *cum* substantial redistribution were overcome.

There is no doubt whatsoever that the ANC will win the upcoming 1999 elections. It faces no opposition of practical importance. The National Party will not obtain the same number of seats as they did in 1994. Rather, it is a party on its way out, one with a severely stained historical record, and Inkatha will never be anything but an ethnic party – a party whose fate furthermore is completely dependent on a single person. It is far more doubtful whether the victor in the 1999 elections will be able to improve the present situation very much. The international economy may well enter a period of lower growth in the wake of the Asian crisis, which means that not only will the South African government be as hard pressed as before to come up with a credible growth strategy, but it will also have to deliver the goods in a much more unfavorable external setting. At the same time it will also have to design its strategy in such a way that it will be possible to bridge not only the historical gap caused by past racial discrimination but also the quickly widening gap between the currently employed and un-employed.

**Notes**

1    See Lundahl and Ndlela (1980) and Lundahl (1982) for details.
2    For economic analyses of apartheid, see e.g. Porter (1978), Lipton (1985), Lundahl (1992) and Lowenberg and Kaempfer (1998).
3    A recent work on the Nationalist era is that of O'Meara (1996).
4    Notably Johnson (1977). For criticisms of Johnson's view, see e.g. the essays in Brewer (1989).
5    Cf. the references in note 1.
6    Lipton (1985), p. 307.
7    Charney (1987), p. 8.
8    For the Botha presidency, see e.g. Schrire (1992).
9    For details, see e.g. Ottaway (1993), Sparks (1995) and Sisk (1995).
10   Schrire (1992), p. 111.
11   The speech is reproduced as Appendix B in op.cit.
12   Sisk (1995), p. 4.
13   Ibid., Chapter 3 and p. 14.
14   See Lundahl and Petersson (1996) for an analysis of NEDLAC procedures and problems.
15   Department of Finance (1998a).
16   Department of Finance (1998b).
17   Department of Finance (1998a).
18   Ibid.
19   Ibid., Department of Finance (1998b).

## References

Brewer, John D. (ed.) (1989), *Can South Africa Survive? Five Minutes to Midnight*. Macmillan: Basingstoke.

Charney, Craig (1987) 'The National Party, 1982-1985: A Class Alliance in Crisis', in: Wilmot G. James (ed.), *The State of Apartheid*. Lynne Rienner Publications: Boulder, CO.

Department of Finance, Republic of South Africa (1998a), *1998/99 Budget*. 31 March. Pretoria.

Department of Finance (1998b), *Quarterly Review*. 16 November. Pretoria.

Johnson, R.W. (1977), *How Long Will South Africa Survive?* Macmillan: London and Basingstoke.

Lipton, Merle (1985), *Capitalism and Apartheid: South Africa, 1910-84*. Gower: Aldershot.

Lowenberg, Anton D. and Kaempfer, William H. (1998), *The Origins and Demise of South African Apartheid*. University of Michigan Press: Ann Arbor, MI.

Lundahl, Hanna and Petersson, Cecilia (1996), *NEDLAC: A Boxing Ring or a Negotiating Forum*. Lund University, Department of Political Science: Lund.

Lundahl, Mats (1989), 'Apartheid: Cui Bono?' *World Development*, Vol. 17.

Lundahl, Mats (1992), *Apartheid in Theory and Practice: An Economic Analysis*. Westview Press: Boulder, CO.

Lundahl, Mats and Ndlela, Daniel B. (1980), 'Land Alienation, Dualism, and Economic Discrimination: South Africa and Rhodesia', *Economy and History*, Vol. 23.

O'Meara, Dan (1996), *Forty Years Lost: The Apartheid State and the Politics of the National Party, 1948-1994*. Ravan Press: Randburg.

Ottaway, David (1993), *Chained Together: Mandela, de Klerk, and the Struggle to Remake South Africa*. Times Books: New York.

Porter, Richard C. (1978), 'A Model of the Southern-African-Type Economy', *American Economic Review*, Vol. 68.

Schrire, Robert (1992), *Adapt or Die: The End of White Politics in South Africa*. Hurst & Company: London.

Sisk, Timothy D. (1995), *Democratization in South Africa: The Elusive Social Contract*. Princeton University Press: Princeton, NJ.

Sparks, Allister (1995), *Tomorrow Is Another Country: The Inside Story of South Africa's Road to Change*. Hill and Wang: New York.

# 2 The South African economy after apartheid

The abolition of the apartheid system in South Africa changes the economic playing field, resolving old problems while creating new ones. Ever since the arrival of the first Europeans in South Africa in 1652 the economic system has been based on the generation of wealth for a small number of people at the expense of the majority of the population. In the 1990s, however, this system started to break down. During the past five or six years South Africa has undergone political change of a magnitude not seen since the whites took command.

This political change will lead to economic change, and a redistribution from the white minority to the African majority is inevitable. It will, however, not be painless.

## The apartheid legacy

Economic growth in South Africa during the first half of the twentieth century was built on a combination of low wages, high capital formation, tariff protection and government intervention. Racial discrimination guaranteed that that the unskilled wage rate was kept down in both mining and agriculture. Capital was imported from abroad. During the 1920s extensive import substitution began in manufacturing and a large public sector was built up.

This policy worked more or less satisfactorily until the 1970s. Thereafter, however, the rate of economic growth slowed and the economy entered a stagnation phase that by and large still persists. The apartheid system was converted from an engine of growth into a brake. Lack of skilled labor interacted with wage increases for unskilled workers, a reduction of the capital inflow and a gradual saturation of the domestic market. The immigration of whites was reduced in a situation where skilled and semi-skilled positions were reserved for people of European extraction. At the same time the labor immigration of Africans from the surrounding nations decreased as a result of political changes in these states. International sanctions reduced investment in South Africa and the skewed distribution of income kept the purchasing power of the masses down.

In the mid-1980s South Africa's GDP per capita was decreasing. The white farmers, who hitherto had been supported by extensive government subsidies, were to an increasing extent forced to rely on market prices and conditions. At the same time it became clear that redistribution of the land to Africans would take place in the not too distant future. Pessimism with respect to the future began to spread. Mining was facing problems as well: increasing costs and stagnating or falling prices. Import substitution led to a domestic reduction of foreign competition, but the domestic industry that had been created displayed low productivity and high costs. In sum, no sector in the economy was doing well.

**The social situation**

Apartheid had distributional effects as well. In every field the white minority had managed to reach a living standard far above that of the African majority and the Asian and Colored minorities. In 1983 white disposable incomes were on average 2.7 times as high as those of Asians, 3.8 times those of Coloreds, 4.6 times those of urban Africans and no less than 16 times those of Africans living in 'areas with no growth', i.e. mainly the bantustans. In 1990 45 percent of the population lived in absolute poverty. The figures for the distribution of wealth and land complete the picture of a white upper class and a mainly African inferior class.

The differences created by the apartheid system can be seen in other ways as well. Statistically, South Africa belongs to the 'upper-middle-income' countries in the World Bank classification. Despite this ranking and the fact that the country produced enough to guarantee a calorie intake which on average was twice as high as the recommended one, malnutrition and deficiency-related diseases were common among the African population, adults as well as children.

The situation was similar in the housing market. In the mid-1980s there was an excess supply of apartments and houses for whites while the Africans living in the townships were forced to crowd 17–20 people into each house (four rooms on average). For the Africans working in 'white' areas the situation was even worse: one million workers had to share 400,000 beds in single-sex hostels. Available figures for water, sanitation, fuel, electricity, etc., point in the same direction.

A third area where racial discrimination left clear traces is health and medicare. Diseases related to poverty were much more common among the non-white groups than among the whites. African death rates by far exceeded white figures, not least for children, and the causes of death were far more related to poverty. Epidemic diseases and tuberculosis were common.

While 25 percent of the whites had some type of post high-school education in 1990, the corresponding figure for Asians was 6.5, for Coloreds 3 and for Africans 0.6 percent. Barely 20 percent of the latter group had any secondary education. Much more was spent on each white child than on children in the other racial groups (seven times as much as on each African child). The quality of the African schools was dismal and 17 percent left these schools before the first year had passed.

Geographically related indicators convey a similar picture. At the end of the 1980s the regions with large bantustan areas performed significantly worse in terms of production and income per capita, life expectancy at birth, number of hospital beds, number of physicians and nurses per 1,000 inhabitants and literacy than areas with a large share of whites in the population.

**Redistribution and growth**

The socially distorting effects of the apartheid system have of course led to strong demands for measures that can remedy the inequitable situation in all the areas listed above. The discriminated groups have waited for a long time without being able to make their voice heard. The social situation in the country is explosive and the new government must demonstrate that it takes the demands seriously. What can be done, then, as far as redistribution is concerned? In the short run the only possibility is the one offered by the government budget. Government revenue may be increased, expenditure may be reduced and, finally, the deficit may be allowed to grow.

None of these three alternatives offer anything but marginal possibilities. In the first place, South Africa is not a low-tax country. This makes it difficult to increase revenue. The total share of taxes in GDP amounted to a little more than 30 percent in 1992. This is a high figure from a global perspective, above average for upper-middle-income countries and just a few percentage points below the figure for the industrial countries. Income taxes, which account for more than two-thirds of total tax revenues, are heavily concentrated to the upper income brackets. The company tax rate, 40 percent, is higher than in most of the countries that South Africa has to compete against in international markets. The value added tax can be increased for luxury goods, but basic necessities will presumably be exempted altogether. Wealth taxes are expensive to administer and will not give rise to substantial revenues. Possibly something can be done via capital gains taxation and excise duties but the conclusion is clear: it is not possible to increase government revenue substantially without an increase in GDP.

On the expenditure side the immediate future looks gloomy as well. It is not possible to redistribute any large sums in favor of the social sectors (education, health, etc.) for the simple reason that it is difficult to find items that can be cut. South Africa already uses a comparatively large share of GDP on health care, housing and – not least – education (while the social insurance system is badly developed).

Within each of these areas it is possible to carry out a redistribution from whites to other ethnic groups, but it is hardly possible to make any drastic improvement for the latter in the short run. The abolition of apartheid does not entail any major gains that may be used for social purposes. The dismantling of the bantustan system will require resources that are at least equivalent to those required for the administration of the system. Reductions in defense spending will presumably be eaten up by expenditure on law and order. The available estimates indicate that no more than two or three percent of GDP may be redistributed in this way.

The alternative then is to underbalance the government budget, i.e. to increase public borrowing. The share of public debt in GDP, around 50 percent in 1994, is a lot lower than, for example, that of Sweden (with over 90 percent), and the share of interest and amortization payments in total government expenditure, a little more than 16 percent in 1992/93, is not alarming. Increasing the public debt does, however, not seem advisable in a situation where interest rates are high both inside and outside the country. The loans taken must be paid back with interest in the future and should hence be used for activities that increase production and exports directly rather than for social purposes. Otherwise, the public debt may quickly increase and a tightening may be necessary in a situation where the economy needs stimulation.

Only marginal redistribution is possible in the short run. For sustained change to be possible the economy must grow. There are, however, no simple recipes for this. Many ideas have been advanced with respect to a 'kickstart'. This is to be achieved by using the increased demand that would be generated by redistributive measures in combination with the excess capacity that exists in a number of branches, notably among small firms. It is, however, very doubtful whether this reasoning holds. The extent of capacity utilization has varied considerably from branch to branch and it is by no means certain that the demand that may be created will be directed towards those sectors that display most excess capacity. Self-sustained growth in the South African economy can be created only in the long run and only if the government can master the macroeconomic stabilization problems.

## Stabilization and recovery

Table 2.1. shows the development of GDP in South Africa from 1986 to 1993. This period was characterized by a recession, and GDP per capita fell. Thereafter, however, it seems as if this trend has been broken and the South African economy now seems to be on the right track. GDP grew somewhat in 1993 (1.2 percent) and the 1994 figure is estimated to be around 2.3 percent. Increased trade and growth in the world economy in combination with increased domestic consumption, improved prospects for agriculture, and increased spending on the social infrastructure will presumably increase the growth rate even more during 1995.

Political unrest may dampen the recovery. Normally, a boom in South Africa is preceded by a build-up of the gold and currency reserves, followed by a reduction of the market interest rates and an increase in the level of investment. Today, however, foreign reserves are small as a result of capital flight, low prices on primary products (although recently the gold price has increased) and payments related to the foreign debt.

Economic policy as well has served to slow down the recovery. The rate of inflation has been high in South Africa during the past two decades, partially as a result of oil price shocks, increased wages and harvest failures. Since 1989, therefore, combating inflation is at the top of the agenda of the Reserve Bank, with strict monetary policy, high interest rates and a stable nominal rate of exchange as the main weapons. In spite of these steps, the rate of inflation has stubbornly remained high for a long time. Not until 1992 did it began to decrease and in 1993 and 1994 it fell below the ten percent level, to the lowest figure in twenty years.

**Table 2.1**
**The evolution of GDP 1986–1993**

| Year | GDP[1] | Real change % | GDP/capita[2] |
|------|--------|---------------|---------------|
| 1986 | 254,221 | 0.0 | 7,392 |
| 1987 | 259,561 | 2.1 | 7,367 |
| 1988 | 270,463 | 4.2 | 7,494 |
| 1989 | 276,940 | 2.4 | 7,490 |
| 1990 | 276,060 | -0.3 | 7,289 |
| 1991 | 273,249 | -1.0 | 7,043 |
| 1992 | 267,254 | -2.2 | 6,724 |
| 1993 | 273,311 | 1.2 | 6,640 |

*Source:* South African Department of Finance Mission in Europe
[1] million rand
[2] 1990 prices

The nominal rate of interest remains high despite the lower rate of inflation. The result is increased real lending rates – around 9 percent in 1994. The reason is that the continued outflow of capital tends to reduce the currency reserves. The high interest level will continue until the negative capital flows have turned positive, i.e. until the value of exports increases or foreign capital starts arriving in a steady flow.

Traditionally, South Africa has been a net importer of capital. This, however, ceased to be the case in the mid-1980s. Political turmoil led to large outflows and simultaneously the cost of borrowing abroad rose. When the foreign banks in 1985 began to call in their outstanding loans the debt crisis was on. Since then the balance of payments has constituted a serious obstacle to economic growth in South Africa. In order to finance debt payments the country has been forced to maintain a surplus on the current account and hence to keep imports down. This, in turn, has hit the manu-facturing sector, which is strongly dependent on imported inputs. During the third quarter of 1994, however, it looked as if South Africa was heading back to its traditional position – for the first time in nine years.

It will probably be more difficult for South Africa to maintain a surplus on the current account in the future. Increased growth rates will lead to increased imports. At the same time the incentives to increase exports will be reduced. During the recession exports have been made possible largely by unutilized capacity and no productivity increases that would strengthen the international competitiveness of the country have taken place within the export sectors.

As a result of joining GATT South Africa will furthermore have to re-move the export support that has contributed to the export success of recent years. Import liberalization in combination with an expected real appreciation of the currency will in all probability also increase imports.

The gold and currency reserves have decreased during the past two-three years as a result of capital outflow in the wake of the uncertain political situation. After the April 1994 elections, however, capital inflow has con-tributed to a considerable improvement of the situation. This is important since the reserves, both in 1993 and in 1994, did not even correspond to six weeks' imports – to be compared to the three-month target of the Reserve Bank, which, however, has not been met since 1981.

**Development strategies**

The growth of GDP in South Africa has on average amounted to 0.8 percent per annum during the past decade. In order to bring about an increase to at least 4 percent during the rest of the 1990s, to make possible a higher standard of living, a more equitable distribution and reduced unemployment, the economy must grow by at least 10 percent per year. If, in addition, it is taken into account that the existing production apparatus depreciates, gross investment must increase from 18 percent today to 25 percent.

The question then arises as to how this increase is to be financed. Average domestic savings in South Africa fell short of 20 percent of GDP between 1989 and 1992. An annual net outflow of capital on the order of 2–3 percent of GDP during the same period, combined with an increasing government budget deficit, has reduced the supply of funds for domestic investment even more. The consequence is that domestic savings have fallen short of the desirable gross investment level by 6–7 percentage points. This gap must be closed if a powerful development program is to be launched.

The Reconstruction and Development Programme (RDP) of the ANC, which is the document that will presumably be the main foundation of the development strategy during the next few years, by and large is a basic needs program where public investment in inexpensive housing and infrastructure in lagging areas is to stimulate economic growth and employment. The most important points are: free and compulsory ten-year education, one million new dwellings in five years and improved health care for the majority (with emphasis on preventive care). The RDP is expected to provide employment opportunities for 2.5 million people during the next ten years.

Reconstruction is estimated to cost 80 billion rand, to be taken from the government budget. Tax increases that distort resource allocation are to be avoided and the tax system will be made more efficient. MERG (Macroeconomic Research Group), a network of South African researchers who wrote an economic policy document that served as an important input in the RDP, argues that public projects initially should be financed by borrowing. In the longer run, the idea is that a dynamic policy for trade and industry in combination with the development of South Africa's human capital should increase the productivity of the economy and hence create incentives for private investment and boost exports.

This strategy, however, has to cope with at least two problems. In the first place, it is uncertain how large the productivity increases resulting from public measures will be. Second, it is also uncertain how much time will be required before it is possible to harvest the fruits of the policy.

What is certain is that the main part of the program requires financing in the short run. The scope for an expansive fiscal policy is, however, limited. The budget deficit for the fiscal year ending 31 March 1995 is estimated to amount to 6.6 percent of GDP. The public debt, as we already know, amounted to a little more than half the GDP in 1994. This is not an alarming level. On the contrary, the figure is better than that of most countries of the European Union. Nevertheless, public expenditure that does not generate growth will make it difficult to lower interest rates and hence act as a brake on investment. The interest payments that result from a continued increase of the public debt will in addition reduce the scope for an expansive fiscal policy in the future.

## Trade and industry policy

An important part of the development strategy of the new South Africa is a trade and industry policy that is more outward-looking than hitherto. This is motivated partly by expected efficiency gains, if manufacturing is exposed to competition from abroad, and partly by the need for export revenue to finance imports of inputs and payments of interest and amortization on the foreign debt. However, increasing exports is no simple affair. The level of production costs in South Africa makes it difficult to compete. Inputs, labor and capital are all expensive and productivity is low. In addition, South Africa has problems with respect to flexibility and punctuality of deliveries. In the somewhat longer run, the competitiveness of the manufacturing sector is completely dependent on productivity-increasing investments in human and physical capital as well as in technological developments.

To stimulate growth it is important to create as high a value added as possible within the export sector. It will then be natural to process raw materials that are abundant in South Africa. Hence, large-scale, export-oriented projects have been launched in the steel and aluminum sectors. The idea is that in due time this will stimulate other branches as well as the economy as a whole.

The problem, however, is that the strategy presupposes both capital and skilled labor – production factors that are scarce in South Africa. In addition South African business is characterized by high concentration and a lack of developed networks between companies. This will presumably limit the positive spread effects from this type of effort. Another problem is that pricing policy in South Africa hardly provides incentives for increased processing of raw materials. In most sectors the South African producers pay 20–30 percent more for raw materials than their European competitors and 40 percent more than their competitors in Asia.

MERG advocates an active industrial policy in order to avoid failures during the transition to a more outward-oriented economy. The institutional framework must be investigated and networks in the economy must be strengthened. The state is to facilitate the allocation of investment to the most productive parts of the economy and ensure that the investments made are in line with the needs of the new South Africa. MERG also favors government influence over production decisions and pricing policy within the minerals sector, as well as regulations within construction. Competition legislation will also be overhauled.

Trade policy decisions are to be made jointly by the business community, the trade unions and the government. This will make the implementation of the new policy easier. Concern has, however, been expressed with respect to the weight that MERG wants to place on the bureaucratic process in the new strategy. The South African labor and capital markets are distorted as a result of previous regulations, notably import substitution and apartheid, and this makes efficient decision making harder. In a situation where the knowledge and experience of the bureaucrats are limited and the expectations with respect to the democratic process are great, there is a patent risk that short-sighted, 'political' decisions will be made, rather than decisions that favor long-term growth. These types of decisions seldom favor the poor. The African middle class, rather than the African poor, will increase its influence in the new South Africa. If the latter group is to benefit, long-run growth is a necessary precondition.

## The central role of the economic actors

Private investment, both foreign and domestic, constitutes the key to growth in South Africa. However, as has already been pointed out, the investment picture is complicated by both high interest rates and regulations in the capital market. The fundamental obstacle to growth, however, is the uncertainty that prevails among investors with respect to future economic and social policy. The new South African government must create a climate that suits the market. This requires stability in government finances.

Even though the emphasis of the democratic polity on domestic demand has met with resistance in business circles, the reaction to the new economic policy is generally positive among the actors in the market. They have been pleased by the fact that the democratic movement has put ideas about nationalization, tax increases and consumption-driven growth into the background. The question, however, remains whether the assumption that the state is capable of carrying out productivity-increasing investments – a completely decisive assumption – is a valid one. If not, a higher investment volume will be required if growth is not to be jeopardized and the current account of the balance of payments is not to be weakened.

It is furthermore legitimate to ask the question of whether government control is conducive to private investment. Given the importance that private investment has for the South African economy, this question is completely central. MERG has suggested that a government Capital Issues Commission

28

be set up with a mandate to look into and approve new company issues of financial instruments. It is, however, hardly probable that the government has the ability to create an optimal allocation of resources in this way. It is not at all inconceivable that government interventions of this type will hamper the private will to invest – and without a private will to invest the South African economy is not likely to get back on its feet for a long time.

# 3 The economy of transition: South Africa at the turn of the century

## Problems of stagnation and distribution

In the 1970s South Africa changed from a high-growth to a low-growth economy.[1] During the previous century the rate of growth appears to have been one of the fastest in the world. National income grew by 5–6 percent per annum in real terms from the beginning of the 1920s to the end of the 1960s, driven by a high rate of capital formation, constant real wages as a result of discrimination in the labor market and tariff protection of the manufacturing sector. Before World War II the growth impulses were generated mainly in the mining sector. During the post-war period manufacturing gradually took over this role.

By the mid-1970s, however, much of the hitherto existing dynamism in the South African economy had been lost. The import substitution policy no longer had any role to play. The domestic market for industrial goods was saturated. For expansion to continue incomes had to increase, preferably across a wide spectrum of the population, but this was effectively prevented by the apartheid system. Real wages had begun to increase. Racial discrimination in the labor market created bottlenecks in terms of skilled and semi-skilled labor. Apartheid had turned into a brake on economic growth.

The rate of capital formation decreased as well. South Africa had been a net importer of capital since the 1940s, but when Angola and Mozambique became independent states and political unrest broke out after the Soweto riots in the mid-1970s the balance of payments became a factor that retarded growth. At the same time both private and public foreign lending increased until, in 1985, the foreign banks – mainly for political reasons – demanded repayment. South Africa became a net capital exporter and the domestic savings failed to finance capital formation to the extent required for the high rate of growth to continue.

The growth of real GDP fell from an annual average of 4.3 percent in the 1950s and 5.8 percent in the 1960s to 2.6 percent on average in 1970–85.[2] The South African economy was heading for stagnation. Between 1986 and 1993 GDP grew by a mere 0.8 percent per annum in real terms, which in turn implied that GDP per capita was falling.[3]

While the economy was stagnating another problem was getting increasing attention. Racial discrimination within the South African economic system had generated an income distribution that was the most uneven in the world. The Gini coefficient[4] for South Africa was 0.65 in 1993 – a figure that should be compared with e.g. 0.32 for Sweden or 0.28 for Japan.[5] That year the average income of Africans amounted to a mere 8.5 percent of what the whites earned, that of the Coloreds to 19.6 percent and that of the Asians to 40 percent. No less than 35 percent of all South African households (47 percent in the case of Africans) found themselves below what was defined as the 'minimum living level'.[6]

These income differences are reflected in other indicators as well: wealth, food consumption and nutrition, access to housing and housing standards, access to water and energy, health and access to health care, education, etc.[7] It does not matter which indicator you choose. All of them point unequivocally to an economic structure and a welfare distribution that are both strongly biased in favor of the whites and against the other ethnic groups, notably the Africans.

**The scope for redistribution**

Redistribution is the central issue in the changing economic politics of South Africa. The introduction of political democracy has made it possible for the African majority to argue forcefully in favor of a redistribution on all levels from whites to Africans. The time has come to abolish the injustice that has accumulated over the course of the centuries. What possibilities, then, exist when it comes to redistribution in the short and the long run?

In the short run redistribution must take place via the government budget, i.e. through increased government revenue, through a redistribution of expenditure, or through increased public borrowing. None of these three ways, however, allow for but limited measures. South Africa is not a low-tax country, and increasing the tax revenue in principle presupposes an increased GDP per capita. At the end of the 1980s the tax share of GDP was at the same level as in other middle-income countries.[8]

The high- and middle-income earners already shoulder the highest income tax burden in South Africa. In the mid-1980s over 70 percent came from the 5 percent that had the highest incomes.[9] Company taxes are high as well: 35 percent plus another 25 percent on distributed profits. It is also difficult to increase indirect taxation. The 10 percent value added tax that was introduced in 1991 led to protests from the trade unions and the government had to make an exception for basic foodstuffs.

The alternative to increased tax revenue is increased borrowing, i.e. underbalancing the budget and increasing the public debt. This way as well may be a difficult one to tread. At the end of 1994 the public debt amounted to 55.4 percent of GDP.[10] From a global perspective this is not a high figure.[11] The Government of National Unity, however, emphasizes the importance of fiscal discipline when it comes to creating a good investment climate. Although for example the World Bank argues that South Africa is 'underborrowed' – the foreign share in the total public debt is a mere 3.4 percent[12] – it is hardly probable that a future redistribution will be financed by borrowing.

The third alternative is to redistribute government expenditure. This as well is likely to run into problems. At the end of the 1980s South Africa spent a relatively high share of GDP on health care, housing and education.[13] This expenditure was highly unevenly distributed between the different ethnic groups.[14] Redistribution will thus be inevitable but it will not be possible to increase social spending to the 'white' level for all groups. Taking the 1986/87 budget as the point of departure this would require an almost fivefold increase for the Africans and a threefold increase of total social spending.[15] In the short run this is impossible. The only solution consists in reducing the white standard while simultaneously increasing the level for the other ethnic groups.

A question that has been intensively debated in South Africa is whether it is possible to redistribute the expenditure formerly spent on the administration of the apartheid apparatus, with all its duplications. Here as well, however, the dividend will be low: a maximum of 2 percent of GDP and probably rather 1 than 2 percent.[16] To this may be added around 1 percent through reduced defense outlays. Altogether this implies 2–3 percent of the 1991/92 GDP over a five-year period.[17]

**The RDP**

It is clear that the scope for short-run redistribution is limited. A necessary condition for a sustained improvement of the living standard for the majority of the South African population is that the economy grows. Redistribution must take place at the margin, out of the growing part of the pie. There is almost a consensus with respect to this in contemporary South Africa and this knowledge constitutes one of the pillars of the Reconstruction and Development Programme (RDP)[18] that was the backbone of the election campaign of the ANC in 1994, and which after the elections was taken over in its entirety by the new Government of National Unity.

One of the most important goals of the reconstruction program is to gradually increase the annual growth rate until it reaches 5 percent at the beginning of the 2000s and 300,000 new jobs are created every year. To make this possible the government will change the trade and industry policy. The tariff level will be reduced, the present export support program will be scrapped, small and medium-sized firms will be supported, the technological level will be increased, the labor force will receive education and training, and incentives for private investment will be created.

The new growth strategy is to make it possible to reach the redistribution targets that constitute the basic needs component of the program. This component focuses on infrastructure: one million new dwellings in five years, free and compulsory ten-year education, electricity to 2.5 million households, running water and toilets to one million families and improved health care and medicare for the masses, especially preventive primary health care.

The Reconstruction and Development Programme does not provide any clear indication with respect to how the basic needs package is to be financed. It is, however, clear that the purpose is to reallocate public expenditure rather than increase it. Tax increases that are conducive to distortions of the resource allocation are to be avoided and the efficiency of tax collection is to increase. Inflationary borrowing is out of the question.

**Growth and economic policy**

How can the economic growth that is needed for redistribution be created? There are no panaceas. On the contrary, problems are likely to arise both in the short and the long run. The year 1994 reflected a recovery for the economy of South Africa, with a real GDP growth of 2.4 percent.[19] Most South African economists agree that the most probable figure for the next few years is on the order of 2.5–3 percent.

This is not a glorious figure. There is, however, nothing to guarantee that even this prediction will come true. On the contrary: in the short run there is a risk that growth will be slowed down by economic policy measures that force the economy into a new recession, unless positive expectations are created in private business circles. Expectations that are strong enough to lead to a capital inflow from abroad.

The problem is the following. When the growth rate increases, demand will increase as well, including the demand for imports – in 1994 by 6 percent in real terms.[20] South Africa is simultaneously carrying out considerable tariff and export subsidy reductions. Hence, the current account of the balance of payments, and with that the currency, is under pressure both from the import and the export side. If the currency depreciates, inflation may be imported via higher prices on foreign inputs.

In this situation, the South African Reserve Bank will probably increase the interest rate in order to put a brake on price increases. The Department of Finance will then be forced to conduct a more restrictive fiscal policy; otherwise, the interest rate increases easily lose their impact. Aggregate demand will therefore slacken and with that GDP and employment. Recessive tendencies will spread and in their wake social turmoil easily ensues, even more so as the 1999 elections draw nearer. Recession and social unrest in turn make it difficult to maintain capital inflow from abroad – the capital inflow needed to cover the deficit on the current account.

The independence of the Reserve Bank has been written into the provisional constitution that was forged before the 1994 elections. Under the powerful leadership of Chris Stals, who is known as a 'hard-core' monetarist, the bank has proved though its actions that this independence is real. The question is whether Stals can be made to live with a slightly higher rate of inflation, given that growth is not slowed down. Investors can probably accept 10–12 percent as long as they see that the economy grows and that the government is seriously committed to reducing the budget deficit and controling public spending.

On the other hand, it would be risky to let go too much. The overriding growth problem is that of creating an atmosphere of confidence and belief in the future among investors. An economic environment must be created that is both stable and transparent: an environment where the signals are clear and no drastic, unexpected turnarounds take place. In this process the Reserve Bank has an important role as a 'thug', should the need arise.

## Wage formation and stagflation

Another threat to growth comes from the process of wage formation. The South African trade unions face a difficult problem. They not only have to speak for those who are already employed but also for those who are formally unemployed. The latter group is large, perhaps 40 percent of the labor force, and not even one in ten of those who enter the labor market every year will succeed.[21]

Demanding wage increases under these circumstances may easily worsen the employment situation, but the South African labor market displays clear insider-outsider characteristics, i.e. those who are already 'inside' are given priority by the trade unions over those who remain outside,[22] and these insiders are pushing for higher wages. In the worst case, the result will be that growth turns into stagflation. A higher wage increases consumption as the purchasing power of the workers increases while investment is held back because company profits are lowered. Bottlenecks arise while simultaneously imports increase and exports are reduced by increasing production costs. The balance of payments and the currency are threatened, the price level increases, and the Reserve Bank slams the brakes, aided by the Department of Finance.

Hopefully, the stagflation scenario does not materialize. During the years that passed between the release of Nelson Mandela from prison in 1990 and the elections in 1994 South Africa developed a consensus culture. One of the driving forces in this process was the Congress of South African Trade Unions (COSATU).[23] At the same time the economic recession severely limited wage bargaining and militant socialism faced an ideological crisis after the fall of communism in Eastern Europe. The consensus mode of thinking appears to have been preserved after the elections. Thus, the parties concerned, notably the employers, the trade unions and the state, are intent on foregoing certain demands, provided that they get others instead. The relation between macroeconomic stability, growth, wage formation and redistribution is clear and COSATU has increasingly stressed the importance of influence over macroeconomic policy making and distribution policies. Hopefully, such influence implies that wage demands are kept within the scope offered by the development of productivity, but then it is also necessary that the implementation of important areas of the RDP begins in the near future.

## Growth through redistribution?

Monetary policy and wage demands pose threats to growth mainly in the short run – the growth that results from an economic upturn. Although it has been possible to neutralize these threats in South Africa, it remains unclear whether growth will continue over a longer period. A great deal more is required, especially a well thought-out growth strategy.

Much of the growth debate in South Africa has been concerned with how to get a quick start. An idea that was popular at the beginning of the 1990s was that of basing industrialization on the domestic market. This was to be achieved through a redistribution via government projects concentrated on cheap housing and employment creation.[24] The construction sector at the time was characterized by excess capacity, it was labor-intensive and it was based on domestic production factors. Thus, in the initial phase it would be possible to avoid both inflation and balance of payments problems.

The problem, however, is what would happen next. An expansion within the construction sector would in turn lead to increased demand for intermediate goods from sectors that do not necessarily have excess capacity, are not necessarily labor-intensive and use imported inputs. Thus, the strategy is not without problems. There are risks both in terms of inflation and the balance of payments. The idea of an expansion of the construction sector, however, remains in the Reconstruction and Development Programme, although it is not seen primarily as a generator of growth.

A variation on the same theme – cherished not least by the ANC – is that a redistribution in favor of less well off groups would create a demand pattern that fits the existing production structure in South Africa better and in addition would focus the industrial policy on the stimulation of production of basic necessities.[25] If this is to succeed it is necessary that the structure of production, especially within manufacturing, accommodates itself to the changes in demand. This, however, is likely to run into problems. Hitherto the South African economy has been rather inflexible. New small firms presumably have an advantage in this respect. It is, however, far from clear that the demand that is generated through the redistribution will be directed primarily towards industrial goods produced by small-scale low-cost firms.[26]

The opposite theme – redistribution through growth – has also been discussed, particularly in business circles and within the Nationalist political establishment. Economic policy would then be directed towards the maximization of production and incomes. The problem, however, is that with realistic assumptions with respect to the growth rate (2.5 percent) over a ten-year period, the incomes of the Africans would increase by no more than approximately one percentage point per annum.[27] Hence, growth must be combined with redistributive measures if the least privileged groups are to close the gap between themselves and the most privileged.

**The long-term strategy**

The crystallizing long-term strategy is based on an outward-looking trade policy, to a much larger extent than has hitherto been the case. We have already discussed the problems created by the import substitution policy from the 1970s onwards and the knowledge that the role of minerals, notably gold, as an engine of development has come to an end; these factors together have initiated a change of trade policy. South Africa is presently dismantling its system of export subsidies and reducing the tariff structure in line with GATT requirements.[28]

A reorientation is necessary. The import substitution policy has reached the end of the road and turned into an obstacle for economic development. However, South Africa is facing a new problem: that of finding sectors that in the future may become competitive in the world market. At the same time, the transition to an export-oriented economy will have negative employment consequences in the sectors that were protected before, especially the motor industry, electric appliances, clothes and textiles.[29]

South Africa's exports are dominated by raw materials, notably gold, and by manufactures representing a relatively low value added.[30] Gold production has had to wrestle with high costs and the importance of the sector has decreased during the last several years. The low value added in manufacturing implies that South Africa exports primarily to markets whose share of world trade is decreasing. For increased, export-led, growth a reorientation towards rapidly growing markets is necessary, i.e. products with a higher average value added. South Africa possesses abundant labor but in the international perspective the wage level is high in relation to labor productivity. The country therefore has problems competing with more efficient low-wage countries e.g. in Asia.

A strategy that has been advocated by an increasing number of people in recent years is processing of, for example, minerals. As part of this strategy South Africa has made large-scale investments in, for example, steel and aluminum manufacturing with a view to arriving at further processing later on. This is, however, not a problem-free strategy, as steel and aluminum are branches that are both capital- and skill-intensive and there is a lack of both capital and educated people in South Africa.

The South African economy is dominated by a relatively small number of companies – those that account for most exports. In addition, the system of subcontractors is weakly developed. As a result the export drive must be combined with industrial policy, on the one hand in the form of industrial clusters, to develop networks capable of employment creation and construction of efficient networks of subcontractors and on the other hand in the form of an increased competitive pressure in the economy that serves to reduce costs and increase efficiency. (It is in this light that the dismantling of protection and export subsidies should be seen.) Small and medium-sized firms will also receive assistance with respect to technological development, marketing, physical infrastructure and education.

## The future

The redistribution targets contained in the Reconstruction and Development Programme require growth in order to materialize. The scope for re-distribution via the government budget is limited. At the same time there is no simple road to growth. The dynamism that characterized the South African economy from the time of the mineral discoveries during the late nineteenth century until the 1970s was to a large extent artificial. It built on a combination of protectionism and racial discrimination in the labor market.

The most recent twenty-year period has instead been characterized by low growth rates and stagnation. Import substitution turned into a dead end when the domestic market had been saturated and the apartheid system increasingly turned out to be an anachronism in relation to the economic structure that developed after World War II. It became a brake.

There are many obstacles to future growth. The stabilization policy and the wage formation process may easily pose difficulties in the short run. No panacea exists that is capable of quickly putting the wheels in motion. The economy is facing the prospect of structural changes that will require time. It will gradually be opened to international competition. The challenge then is that of developing sectors where demand is growing fast and where South Africa is capable of holding its own in relation to other nations.

This is no easy task. The protected life that has characterized the South African economy for a long time has led to low productivity at all levels, and the political situation has not yet stabilized enough for South Africa to stand out as an attractive country for investors. An outward-looking trade regime does not automatically lead to increased investment. Both domestic and foreign companies have so far assumed a wait-and-see attitude. In the initial stage public investment will presumably play a relatively important role. This is clearly indicated in the Reconstruction and Development Programme. Public investment must, however, be financed, and the scope for budgetary maneuvers is limited. An increase in private capital formation is therefore crucial for growth. The road to growth is via increased political and economic stability.

## Notes

1   Lundahl, Fredriksson and Moritz (1992).
2   Ibid., p. 309.
3   South African Reserve Bank (1995), pp. 128–29.
4   The Gini coefficient measures the extent of income inequality in a country. It may vary between 0, with national income completely evenly distributed, and 1 (maximum concentration).
5   The ten countries in the world that have the most equal distributions lie somewhere between 0.20 and 0.35 (Todaro (1989), p. 152).
6   Whiteford, Posel and Kelatwang (1995), pp. 21, 15, 5. The minimum living level is defined as the lowest income that the members of a family need in order to remain healthy, have an acceptable hygienic standard and enough clothes for their needs. Calculated per family it is the lowest sum that is required for a family of a given size to be able to live under the social conditions that exist in South Africa (Whiteford and McGrath (1994), p. 59).
7   Wilson and Ramphele (1989), Lundahl and Moritz (1994), pp. 142–50.
8   Lachman and Bercuson (1992), p. 29.
9   Loots (1991), p. 46.
10  South African Department of Finance Mission in Europe (1995), p. 10.

11  The Swedish public debt in 1995 amounted to about 90 percent of GDP (Regeringens proposition 1994/95:100, p. 32).
12  South African Department of Finance Mission in Europe (1995), p. 10.
13  Lachman and Bercuson (1992), p. 21.
14  Lundahl and Moritz (1994).
15  van der Berg (1991), p. 76, Mitra (1992), pp. 138–39.
16  van der Berg (1991), p. 80.
17  Loots (1992), pp. 473–74.
18  ANC (1994).
19  South African Department of Finance Mission in Europe (1995), p. 2.
20  Nattrass (1994), p. 10.
21  Nattrass (1992), p. 1.
22  Lindbeck and Snower (1988).
23  Nattrass (1994), p. 1.
24  Standish (1992).
25  ANC (1990).
26  Standish (1992), p. 121, Moll (1991), p. 323.
27  van der Berg and Siebrits (1991).
28  Hirsch (1995), pp. 50–54.
29  Kotzé (1994).
30  South African Department of Finance Mission in Europe (1994), p. 6.

**References**

ANC (African National Congress) Department of Economic Policy (1990), *Discussion Document on Economic Policy*. September. Johannesburg.

ANC (African National Congress) (1994), *The Reconstruction and Development Programme*. Umanyano Publications: Johannesburg.

Hirsch, Alan (1995), 'From the GATT to the WTO: The Global Trade Regime and its Implications for South Africa', in Mills, Greg; Begg, Alan and van Nieuwkerk, Anthoni (eds), *South Africa in the Global Economy*, South African Institute of International Affairs: Johannesburg.

Kotzé, P.E. (1994), *Reform of the Protective System*, April 1994/1. Industrial Development Corporation of South Africa: Sandton.

Lachman, Desmond and Bercuson, Kenneth, with Daudi Ballalli, Robert Corker, Charalambos Christofides, and James Wein (1992), *Economic*

*Policies for a New South Africa,* IMF Occasional Paper No. 91, Washington, D.C.

Lindbeck, Assar and Snower, D. (1988), *The Insider-Outsider Theory of Employment and Unemployment.* MIT Press: Cambridge, MA and London.

Loots, Lieb J. (1991), 'A Tax Strategy for Redistribution', in Moll, Peter, Nattrass, Nicoli and Loots, Lieb (eds), *Redistribution: How Can It Work in South Africa?* David Philip: Cape Town.

Loots, Lieb J. (1992), 'Budgeting for Post-Apartheid South Africa', in Moss, Glenn and Obery, Ingrid (eds), *South African Review 6: From "Red Friday" to CODESA.* Ravan Press: Johannesburg.

Lundahl, Mats and Moritz, Lena (1994), 'The Quest for Equity in South Africa - Redistribution and Growth', in Odén, Bertil *et al., The South African Tripod: Studies on Economics, Politics and Conflict.* Scandinavian Institute of African Studies: Uppsala.

Lundahl, Mats, Fredriksson, Per and Moritz, Lena (1992), 'South Africa 1990: Pressure for Change', in Lundahl, Mats, *Apartheid in Theory and Practice: An Economic Analysis.* Westview Press: Boulder, CO.

Mitra, Raja J. (1992), 'Public Expenditure and Finance Issues in South Africa'. Draft 21 January. World Bank: Washington, D.C.

Moll, Terence (1991), 'Growth through Redistribution: A Dangerous Fantasy?', *South African Journal of Economics,* Vol. 59.

Nattrass, Nicoli (1992), *Profits and Wages: The South African Economic Challenge.* Penguin Books: London.

Nattrass, Nicoli (1994), 'South Africa: The Economic Restructuring Agenda - A Critique of the MERG Report', *Third World Quarterly,* Vol. 5.

Regeringens proposition (1994/95:100). *Bilaga 1. Finansplanen.* Stockholm: Riksdagens tryckeriexpedition.

South African Department of Finance Mission in Europe (1994), *The South African Economy in Brief.* December. Zürich.

South African Reserve Bank (1995), Quarterly Bulletin. March 1995, No. 195. Pretoria.

Standish, Barry (1992), 'Resource Endowments, Constraints and Growth Policies', in Abedian, Iraj and Standish, Barry (eds.), *Economic Growth in South Africa: Selected Policy Issues.* Oxford University Press: Cape Town.

Todaro, Michael P. (1989), *Economic Development in the Third World.* 4th edition. Longman: New York and London.

van der Berg, Servaas (1991), 'Prospects for Redistribution of Primary and Secondary Incomes in the Transition to Democracy', Unpublished paper, Conference of the Economic Society of South Africa. Stellenbosch, 2-3 October.

van der Berg, Servaas and Siegbrits, Krige (1991) 'Redistribution and Growth', Paper to a Workshop of the Economic Trends Group, Cape Town, 22-24 November.

Whiteford, Andrew and McGrath, Michael (1994), *The Distribution of Income in South Africa*. Human Sciences Research Council: Pretoria.

Whiteford, Andrew; Posel, Dori and Kelatwang, Teresa (1995), *A Profile of Poverty, Inequality and Human Development*. Human Sciences Research Council: Pretoria.

Wilson, Francis and Ramphele, Mamphela (1989), *Uprooting Poverty: The South African Challenge*. W.W. Norton & Company: New York and London.

# 4 The post-apartheid economy, and after?

Since the title of this chapter may appear somewhat ambiguous, it seems necessary to begin with an explanation of the term 'post-apartheid economy' and to indicate what I understand by the word 'after' in this context. Essentially, 'post-apartheid economy' will be used to designate an economy in transition from the situation that prevailed during the period of Nationalist government from 1948 to 1994 (or perhaps 1990 is a better end-year) to a situation that is still somewhere in the not-so-well-defined future. Since the beginning of the 1990s, the 'post-apartheid economy' has been one of the hottest discussion topics in South Africa. One way or another all South Africans are concerned with the issues of growth and redistribution. The apartheid era is over and the country finds itself in a period of transition, the post-apartheid period, but to what? Here, 'after' will be defined as the period when, if ever, the government led by the African National Congress (ANC) will have reached its development objectives.

We will begin by sketching the situation that the ANC-led government inherited – a picture of the state in which the economy was left as a result of apartheid. Thereafter, we will provide an account of how the economic program of the ANC developed from the vague *Freedom Charter* to the *Reconstruction and Development Programme* in 1994 and the related *Growth, Employment and Redistribution* strategy in 1996. Finally, we will discuss some of the most important difficulties with the strategy that finally emerged – obstacles that must be overcome if the goals are to be attained, i.e. if the 'after' stage is ever to be reached.

### The legacy of apartheid: inequality and inefficiency

The economic legacy of apartheid was twofold: on the one hand income and welfare disparities that were among the largest in the world,[1] and on the other hand an inefficient resource allocation that had severe adverse effects on the growth rate as well.[2] This was the result of a long historical process. Even though the term 'apartheid' was new in 1948, when the National Party triumphed in the parliamentary elections, racial discrimination and far-reaching government intervention in the economy were not. In fact, the unequal treatment of Africans and Europeans began with the very advent of the latter in South Africa in 1652[3] and, viewed in this light, the detailed legal codification that took place after 1948[4] constituted the end of a process rather than the beginning of one. Government intervention was not a new phenomenon. In its 'modern' form this dated back to the mineral discoveries during the last third of the nineteenth century and the need to obtain a labor force at the lowest possible cost; and to the emergence of a class of 'poor whites' around the turn of the century, in the wake of deteriorating economic conditions in the countryside in combination with the devastations of the Boer War.[5]

Still, it cannot be denied that the extent of market-distorting regulations grew substantially after 1948. What the Nationalists created was perhaps not the product of the premeditated 'grand plan' noted by scholars like Pierre van den Berghe, Brian Bunting or Willem de Klerk,[6] but rather a system born in an environment characterized by opposing views, conflicts and compromises, as argued by Deborah Posel.[7] Nevertheless, 'There was clearly some method in the madness of Apartheid'.[8] Posel herself summarizes its extent:

> Building on the foundations laid by previous segregationist regimes, the National Party (NP) government built Apartheid into a monstrously labyrinthine system which dominated every facet of life in South Africa. From its election victory in 1948, the NP steadily consolidated its hold on the state, with a greater degree of ideological fervour than any previous ruling party. Long-standing state controls over the African labour market were restructured and greatly intensified. A national system of labour bureaux, introduced in the 1950s to monitor and control African employment, placed increasingly severe constraints on Africans' freedom of movement and occupational choice. The Population Registration Act (1950), Group Areas Act (1953), Bantu Education Act (1953), Reser-

vation of Separate Amenities Act (1953), and others laid the groundwork for a more rigid and thoroughgoing system of racial domination than had existed to date. Buttressed by a large and powerful arsenal of security laws, the Nationalists also mounted an unprecedented assault on their political enemies. By the early 1960s organised black opposition had been smashed, and would take over a decade to recover. The 1960s then saw the launch of an ambitious and ruthless programme of social engineering, which stripped the majority of Africans of their South African citizenship, and forcibly removed over three and a half million from allegedly 'white' areas of the country to putative ethnic 'home-lands'.[9]

The apartheid system increased the degree of distortion in the labor market. Wage rates differed between racial groups performing the same tasks, non-whites were crowded out of skilled and semi-skilled occupations and the homelands system made it impossible for the market for unskilled labor to clear.[10] Finally, the very creation of the apartheid bureaucracy imposed new costs on the economy, both directly and in the form of rent-seeking by the bureaucrats:

There are few countries that can compare with South Africa in this regard. By 1985 the political system had given birth to 13 Houses of Parliament or Legislative Assemblies, as well as a President's Council with quasi-legislative functions. Occupying seats in these 14 bodies were 1270 members. Each of these legislative organs has executive structures, which by 1986 had spawned 151 departments. These included 18 Departments of Health and Welfare; 14 Departments of Education; 14 Departments of Finance & Budget, and Agriculture and Forestry; 13 Departments of Urban Affairs or Local Government; 12 Departments of Works and Housing; 9 Departments of Economic Affairs or Trade and Industry; 5 Departments of Foreign Affairs, Transport, Post & Tele-graphs, Labour & Manpower, Law & Order, Defence or National Security; 3 Departments of Justice, and 1 Department of Environmental Affairs & Tourism. Finally, these Departments were responsible to 11 Presidents, Prime Ministers or Chief Ministers in South Africa.

Such a network is not cheap to run, not least because it provides security of income and privileges for those who work in it. As time went by, its incumbents developed a powerful interest in keeping the whole system going, whatever ideological goals were being pursued.[11]

Dirigisme was by no means new in Apartheid South Africa, nor was it limited to the labor market. The land market had been formally regulated since the beginning of the century. The 1913 Natives Land Act and the 1936 Native Trust and Land Act limited dramatically the land area at the disposal of the African majority, confining around 70 percent of the population to about 14 percent of the land area, and by no means to the best soils.[12] White farmers received considerable financial subsidies from the government, amounting at times to almost one-fifth of their total income. State marketing boards intervened in the distribution of agricultural produce from producer to consumer (close to 90 percent in the late 1960s) operating various price stabilization schemes in the process.[13]

The industrial sector was affected as well. Beginning in 1928, a number of state-owned corporations were created in strategic areas of manufacturing, such as ISCOR (steel), SASOL (fuel), FOSCOR (phosphate) and ARMSCOR (arms), and the state also took on a direct producer responsibility in such areas as transportation and electricity.[14] These enterprises, which after the Nationalist takeover of government in 1948 increasingly aimed at self-sufficiency in the face of a hostile international opinion, generally produced inefficiently – at a cost which was higher than the level prevailing in the international market.

This inefficiency was to a large extent the result of tariff protection begun in the 1920s, supplemented by quantitative import restrictions after World War II. From 1925 until the beginning of the 1970s, South Africa's foreign trade policy was essentially an inward-looking one, with concentration on import substitution instead of on export promoting measures.[15] In addition, for political reasons (keeping Africans out of white areas), in the 1960s a costly attempt was made to partly decentralize the manufacturing sector into areas bordering the homelands,[16] and in 1982 a Regional Industrial Development Programme was introduced, with special incentives, to promote growth and development in nine so-called 'development regions'.[17] Nothing in terms of employment and development came out of the former,[18] and with respect to the latter Servaas van der Berg offered the following verdict after a decade of operation: 'a clear case of spending that could be slashed by immediately terminating the incentives for all new applicants and giving notice to existing entrepreneurs that these incentives are to be phased out'.[19]

Murali Iyengar and Richard Porter[20] have quantified the impact of apartheid on the efficiency of the South African economy with the aid of a five-sector model of a small, open economy. In this model, which is based on data for 1980, apartheid first of all takes the form of an influx control from bantustans (homelands), where unskilled Africans cultivate the land, to the rest of the (white) economy. Second, a certain percentage of all (unskilled) jobs in mining and in the skilled labor categories of manufacturing and other urban jobs is reserved for whites. (The fifth sector is white agriculture, where only unskilled labor is used.) Third, unskilled white workers are guaranteed full employment at a wage rate which exceeds the African unskilled wage by a given percentage.

The model indicates that the removal of all apartheid restrictions would have increased real GDP by 6–9 percent, depending on how fast Africans were assumed to be able to move into skilled jobs. African bantustan agriculture would have disappeared altogether and the output of white agriculture would have declined as well, since labor would have moved out of that sector into the high-productivity urban pursuits. Mining output would have displayed a slight increase, with Africans taking over jobs from whites, but the main 'winners' would have been manufacturing and other urban production, once the influx control had been removed for both skilled and unskilled African labor.

To the efficiency losses caused by apartheid we must add those resulting from other government policies. What their quantitative impact may have been is impossible to say, but the experience of South Africa with respect to import substitution resembles that of other developing countries[21] strongly:

> poor industrialisation and trade policies in the glorious post-war era nullified an important potential link between industrial exports and economic growth in SA. Economic policy was internally oriented, rather than aimed at success in ballooning world markets, industrial exports received pathetically little attention, and the rand was too strong for industrial exports to be profitable. Hence an array of inefficient direct controls over imports and primary sector wages was needed to keep the balance of payments healthy, while the tariff structure became one of the most complex and intractable in the world. Above all, glorious opportunities for manufacturing export growth and technical progress were frittered away.[22]

During the quarter-century following World War II, between 50 and 90 percent of all imports were made subject to quantitative restrictions.[23] Between 1974 and 1986, the structure of South African protection imposed an implicit export tax averaging 71 percent on all export goods (34 percent if gold is excluded). 'Given the strong incentive to produce for the domestic market, many exporters failed to produce and firms concentrated on the domestic market', summarizes Merle Holden.[24] The results in terms of efficiency left plenty to be desired:

> The import substitution programme was weakened by the lack of export strategy, and the reliance of industry on protection and ever-more advanced machinery imports, hence entrenching the international non-competitiveness of local production, the typical patterns for developing countries with natural resources which have attempted import substitution behind tariff walls. Real manufacturing import levels as percentage of GDP failed to fall, as South Africa moved 'up' the imports scale, requiring increasing inputs of imported machinery, transport equipment and technology to keep industry going. The 'easy' stage of import substitution in local consumer goods, some durables and simpler machinery was basically complete by the early 1970s, with further scope for import-replacement limited to capital and intermediate goods and high-technology sectors.[25]

A number of government commissions in the 1970s pointed to the desirability of making the industrial sector less dependent on tariff protection and more internationally competitive. Little came out of this, however. It was decided to keep the protection and only half-hearted, selective measures were implemented with respect to export promotion.[26]

Also,

> the post-1950 state flops into the incompetent category – witness its efforts to control and steer labour and capital markets which favoured low-productivity sectors (and firms) like agriculture at the expense of modern manufacturing and services, grandiose parastatals aiming at self-sufficiency (led by the troika – Sasol, Iscor and Armscor), poor technology policies, expensive industrial decentralisation failures, ballooning government spending and bureaucracy, and so on.[27]

In particular, the policy with respect to the parastatals appears to have been a clear failure:

> The empirical evidence suggests that policy makers in South Africa responded to sanctions by adopting a proactive, inward-looking strategy. The state interventions in developing Sasol, Atlantis Diesel, and Mossgas

are extreme examples of the distorting effects of this inward policy on the structure of production, and the extreme costs which have been incurred. The impositions of sanctions in and of themselves would have led to price signals in the economy which would have encouraged import substitution anyway. With the benefit of hindsight it could be argued that state intervention was unnecessary, given the selective applications of sanctions and the inability to enforce them globally. The premium paid by South Africa for the sanctioned imports reflected part of the cost of the import substitution which occurred.[28]

Turning to the equality issue, the legacy of apartheid is even clearer. No matter which indicator is used, a completely unequivocal picture emerges, with white living standards far above those of all other races, notably those of the Africans. Thus, in 1980, the per capita income of Asians was around one-fourth of that of whites, that of Coloreds one-fifth and that of Africans one-twelfth.[29] The Gini coefficient of South Africa for 1978 was the highest among those countries for which data were available: 0.66,[30] and the figures reported between 1970 and 1993 consistently lie between 0.65 and 0.71.[31] In the latter year 47 percent of all African households found themselves below the poverty line, against a mere 2 percent of the white households.[32] The African group also accounted for no less than 95 percent of the shortfall between actual incomes and the level which the absolutely poor households would have had to reach for all households to rise above the poverty line.[33]

Other welfare indicators convey exactly the same impression. Malnutrition is a big problem within the African group – both for children and for adults – in spite of the fact that the country regularly produces enough food to ensure a calorie intake which is more than twice as high as the recommended level.[34] Housing conditions are often appalling, with overcrowding, lack of running water, energy and elementary sanitary facilities being quite common in township areas and homelands[35] The incidence of and causes behind mortality and morbidity differ markedly between the various ethnic groups, with whites being best off and Africans worst, diseases related to poverty being far more prevalent among the latter and 'welfare-related' illnesses dominating the picture among the former.[36] When it comes to education, finally, the Bantu Education Act, 'by far the most important and by far the most deadly in its effects' of all the apartheid laws passed during the first years of Nationalist rule,[37] and related legislation made it virtually impossible for Africans to make it further than the primary cycle in low-quality schools, and usually not even that, while the vast majority of the whites at least passed through the secondary stage as well and more than one in four (in 1990) had some kind of tertiary education.[38]

## After the transition: the goals

When Nelson Mandela left prison as a free man in February 1990, the ANC did not have much of an economic program to present to the world.[39] The struggle had been mainly political, the leaders had been either in exile or in jail and few advances had been made on the vague and contradictory formulations of economic strategy presented in the *Freedom Charter* (1988), a document which was by then 35 years old. The *Freedom Charter* called for the nationalization of mines, banks and monopoly industries and for a transfer of land from whites to Africans. At the same time, however, it established the principle of free competition in all sectors and private ownership was by no means ruled out. The vision seems to be that of a mixed economy, with the state playing an important role both as a policy-maker and planner and as a direct producer.

The *Freedom Charter* should be read as a general statement of aspiration rather than as a coherent view of how the economy should be run.[40] However, the lifting of the ban on the ANC in February 1990 and the beginning of negotiations with the National Party made an economic strategy increasingly necessary. As a result, during the next four years an economic program was born – a program which was taken over by the government of national unity after the 1994 elections and which, with some changes, remains in place at the time of writing, after the resignation of the Nationalists from government.

The first steps were taken during two workshops held by the ANC and COSATU (Congress of South African Trade Unions) in Harare in 1990. These, however, produced a document[41] that was as preliminary, vague and contradictory as ever the *Freedom Charter*.[42] In this document the state still plays the role of an efficient guardian that will put the economy on a growth path, boost incomes and employment and enable the satisfaction of basic needs. Although the demise of communism in Eastern Europe had created increased confidence in markets as important tools for creating an efficient economy, the market mechanism (according to this document) has to function within an environment created by state-led development planning, and considerable emphasis is still put on nationalization and collective ownership. Redistribution is seen both as conducive to growth, via a restructuring of demand leading to a creation of mass markets, and as a way of satisfying the basic needs of the population.

During 1990 and 1991 nationalization was gradually put into the background. As it seems, it did not take Mandela more than a few months after being released from prison to change his mind on the subject.[43] Nationalization was seen as one of many possible means that could be used to increase efficiency in the economy, if the circumstances justified it. By and large, however, confusion continued to prevail with respect to the eventual general economic course of the ANC. In 1991 and 1992 another shift took place – away from the idea that growth could be generated through a redistribution of income and wealth that would serve to boost the demand of a vast segment of the population to a belief that it would have to be put at the very center of attention to make redistribution sustainable.[44] The latter year saw the publication of a document that laid down the political guidelines of the ANC[45] where the mixed economy and the private sector received more attention than hitherto and where, by and large, a spirit of pragmatism prevailed.

At the same time, an academic network, the Macroeconomic Research Group (MERG), sympathetic to the political goals of the ANC, was carrying out a series of investigations of various aspects of the South African economy. These investigations – after a long political process – formed the basis for a report which covered all aspects of the economy and which was intended as an input in the policy making of the ANC.[46] The document was hardly coherent, which was no surprise, given the wide-ranging differences in ideological outlook of those involved. Moreover, it displayed some important analytical defects, for example in the discussion of productivity increases, their possible dependence on imported inputs and the possibility that this could lead to a balance-of-payments crisis, as well as in the argumentation in favor of a minimum wage, where it was not taken into account that minimum wages may have negative effects on employment and investment.[47] Still, the MERG document had much in common with what eventually became the official economic strategy of the ANC: the *Reconstruction and Development Programme* (RDP).[48]

Fundamentally, the RDP is a basic needs program. The main targets are: ten years of compulsory education for everybody, at least one million low-cost houses in the next five years, provision of electricity for an additional 2.5 million households by the year 2000, clean water and adequate sanitation for everybody, improved and affordable health, particularly preventive and primary health care for all, and a substantial redistribution of land to the landless in rural areas. Public investments in inexpensive housing and infrastructure in backward areas are envisaged to stimulate economic growth and create employment.

The foundation upon which the satisfaction of the basic needs rests is economic growth. A strategy for industry and trade which includes, among other things, liberalization of imports, increased competition, support to small and medium-sized firms as well as technological development is envisaged to enhance the productivity and competitiveness of the South African economy with the aid of an improved stock of human capital, achieved mainly through education. It is foreseen that this policy will be conducive to increased private investment.

How the RDP is to be financed is not completely clear, but it is stressed that in the longer run the program must be made to fit into the regular budget, i.e. it entails a reallocation rather than an expansion of government expenditure. Tax increases that will distort the resource allocation must be avoided and an effort will be made to make tax collection more efficient. Populist inflationary methods of finance are to be avoided.

The RDP ran into trouble from the very beginning. Its implementation was scheduled to take place through a special RDP fund, financed fundamentally by a reallocation of expenditure from the regular government departments. For 1994/95, 2.5 billion rand were budgeted, to be increased gradually to 12.5 billion in 1998/99. However, due to a lack of spending capacity, especially at the local level, where the administrative machinery was not yet in place, 1.7 billion rand had to be carried over to 1995/96 and it was calculated that at least 20 percent of the RDP budget for the following fiscal year would be spent in 1996/97, at the earliest.[49]

Far more serious, however, was the discovery that the RDP was not feasible in terms of investment.[50] A quantification of the infrastructure requirements in the fields of energy, water, transport, communications, housing, land reform, health, education and security revealed that if the RDP targets were to be met over the five-year period envisaged, public investment in infrastructure would have to grow by 21 percent per annum – a figure above any historical precedent in the country – and the local authorities (mainly the muncipalities) would have to increase their funding of infrastructure by no less than 39 percent on average every year. A (likely) scenario where real GDP grows at 3 percent, the government budget deficit is reduced by 0.5 percentage points every year and private investment increases by slightly more than 7 percent would allow for a yearly growth of public investment in the order of 7.5 percent. Meeting the RDP targets over a period of five years would clearly be impossible.

Plans for a new National Strategy for Growth and Development were announced[51] and work was begun on it.[52] Before these plans could be presented to parliament, however, the RDP office was overtaken by events. In February 1996, the South African Foundation, a lobby for big business, presented its own growth strategy[53] calling for rapid and concerted action in five areas: legislation, macroeconomic policy, government, markets and foreign trade and investment. The approach is largely a supply-side one. In particular, investor confidence has to be boosted through a number of measures if real GDP is to grow by 5–6 percent per annum and employment by 3.5–4 percent. Firm action is needed against crime, the budget deficit has to come down quickly through expenditure reduction, state-owned enterprises must be privatized as soon as possible, the labor market has to be rendered more flexible and regulation must be avoided. Exports should be promoted through the labor market policy, through an exchange rate that makes South Africa competitive internationally and through tax rates that do not differ from those prevailing internationally. Redistribution in favor of the poor, according to this view, comes through increased employment and the increased social spending that is made possible by increasing government revenue in an expanding economy.

The trade unions did not take long to respond with a document stressing job creation and social equity, favoring a much more interventionist policy with concentration on the demand side.[54] The South African Foundation document was seen as a way of dividing society by strengthening the already rich and letting the poor pay for it. The alternative approach suggested by the unions rests on six 'pillars':

1 Jobs can be created through public works, housing programs, expansion of domestic demand, productivity-enhancing training measures, land reform, etc.

2 Social spending on the poor must increase, the rich (including the corporations) must be taxed harder and the value added tax must be lowered on goods consumed by poor people.

3 Anti-trust legislation must be introduced to break up concentration and the monopoly on major economic decision-making.

4   Workers' rights must be promoted.

5   Industrial democracy must be established.

6   Equality and development must be promoted internationally.

The labor movement argues in favor of a slower reduction of the budget deficit so as to avoid deflationary pressures and concomitant reduction of growth and employment creation. Instead, the government should pursue a moderately expansive fiscal policy with expenditure concentrated on redistribution and infrastructure. High wages serve to keep demand up, and training the workers makes them more productive which, in turn, serves to increase output as well, so that inflationary pressure can be kept under control. Once growth is under way private investment will also respond favorably.[55]

In the meantime, the RDP office had been closed and the Department of Finance had taken the lead in the elaboration of a new macroeconomic strategy. This strategy was ready in June 1996. The long-run vision it projects is that:

> As South Africa moves towards the next century, we seek:
> a competitive fast-growing economy which creates sufficient jobs for all work-seekers;
> a redistribution of income and opportunities in favour of the poor;
> a society in which sound health, education and other services are available to all;
> and
> an environment in which homes are secure and places of work are productive.[56]

The government strategy looks a lot more like the South African Foundation approach than like the one suggested by the trade unions.[57] The emphasis is on growth, which is considered as a prerequisite for both employment and redistribution. Unless the growth rate can be increased from 3 to 6 percent per annum at the turn of the century, the unemployment rate will increase substantially, and real aggregate spending on social and community services will grow at a pace barely above that of the population. On the other hand, it is argued, the implementation of the new strategy will make implementation of the RDP 'in all its facets' possible and 400,000 new jobs will be created per annum by the year 2000.[58]

The *Growth, Employment and Redistribution* strategy is for the medium term, as defined up to the year 2000. The supply-side orientation is as evident there as in the *Growth for All* document. Such signals with respect to government behavior that are believed to be received favorably by investors are sent to the private sector. Thus, the fiscal deficit is to be brought down to 4 percent of GDP during 1997/98, instead of to the 4.5 percent envisaged in 1994, to help keep inflation under control. Monetary policy will remain restrictive. Public assets will be 'restructured', i.e. state-owned enterprises will be privatized. In the labor market, a 'structured flexibility within the collective bargaining system', i.e. mainly increased wage flexibility, is aimed for. These are more or less the measures that the business sector has been asking for. The package also attempts to stimulate supply directly, by tax incentives and support to small and medium-scale enterprises. At the same time, however, the speed of tariff reduction will be increased, the real exchange rate will be maintained at a level that ensures international competitiveness and competition policy will be strengthened.

To appease the wage earners, the document points to 'a social agreement to facilitate wage and price moderation, underpin accelerated investment and employment and enhance public service delivery',[59] i.e. in exchange for wage restraint employees should receive guarantees that firms will keep price increases down and increase investment so as to create more jobs, and the government should accelerate spending that increases 'its contribution to social and community living standards' while providing 'a combination of real exchange rate management and tax incentives aimed at encouraging private sector investment'.[60]

The 'integrated' scenario sketched in the government macroeconomic strategy envisages gradually increased GDP growth, as a result of increased domestic and foreign private investment, until a rate of 6.1 percent is reached in 2000, 'increased formal employment until the 400,000 new jobs per annum target is met the same year, coupled with a yearly real wage growth of 1 percent growth in the private sector and less in the public sector', real non-gold export growth above 8 percent on average, a slight increase in gross private savings and a substantial reduction of government dissaving. Altogether this would allow for a fourfold increase of RDP-related spending as compared to the scenario where the present low-growth policy continues.

Pausing for a moment to sum up: on a general level the new economy envisaged (or at least hoped for) by the ANC in the long run is one with a growth of real GDP per capita which is high enough to allow for a substantial redistribution in favor of the poor majority both via the creation of employment and via the expenditure side of the government budget. This economy should be an open one, allowing for a free flow of both goods and factors across the national border. Exports and foreign direct investment are to play a central role when it comes to generating growth, in the setting of a mixed economy dominated by private enterprise. Sound government finances, with expenditures under control and a balanced budget, are projected.


## The transition[61]

The new macroeconomic strategy of the South African government may not be easy to implement. On the most general level, the strategy is based on an econometric model (actually a model taken from the Reserve Bank and devised as a model for monetary policy) and, like all models, the answers it provides to policy questions are simply an outcome of what has been put into it. It may or may not inform the debate. In the worst case, reality may be completely different, something which is important to keep in mind in a country where there are almost as many macroeconometric models as there are economists. It may be very imprudent to base a macroeconomic strategy on one particular model in this situation.

The strategy document puts growth ahead of employment and redistribution, acknowledging that unless the economy grows no employment will be created and there will be nothing to redistribute to the poor. However, it is precisely on the growth side that we find problems with the strategy. The growth-generating forces – investment and exports – are not under the control of the government, and government stabilization policy could easily come into conflict with the growth objective. It is also doubtful whether the strategy will manage to create employment to the extent set out in the document and whether employment will have much effect on poverty.

As is well known, the determinants of investment are difficult to model, and the strategy document of the South African government does not constitute any exception to this rule. In fact, investment does not appear to be based on any explicit investment function but simply on extrapolation of past trends and guesses based on these, both for the private and for the public sector. Public investment in infrastructure is assumed to 'crowd in' private investment to some extent, but more important when it comes to stimulating private investment appears to be such 'positive' signals as determined and coherent macroeconomic policy making, not least increased fiscal discipline, and continued liberalization of the economy. The latter could be achieved through privatization of government-owned enterprises and, on the trade side, through continued and accelerated tariff reduction and the maintenance of an exchange rate which does not overvalue the rand and undermine international competitiveness. A tightening of the fiscal stance, however, also tends to reduce demand and with that the size of the markets for goods and services in which at least those who produce for domestic consumption will have to operate. Unfortunately, whether prospective domestic and international investors pay enough attention to such signals as the size of the budget deficit to guide them in determining their actions or continue their wait-and-see attitude until they see actual sustained growth in the economy is a completely empirical matter and – to make matters even more complicated – one where the South African past has little guidance to offer. History will not absolve the policy makers on this point.

The new strategy foresees that gross domestic investment will increase from 20 percent of GDP to almost 26 percent in the year 2000. For this, it is stated, a capital inflow of close to 4 percent of GDP is required.[62] Again, however, this is a variable outside government control. The crucial decisions are made abroad, in the light of how the South African economy performs in a comparative perspective.

The new macroeconomic strategy envisages a growth of non-gold exports of over 8 percent per annum on average.[63] This is seen as one of the most important growth-generating forces. It is, however, far from clear that the export objective will be attained. Export forecasts are almost as tricky as forecasts of investment in macroeconomic modeling, for the simple reason that small, open economies, like the South African one, by definition have no control over international markets. Thus, exports are an inherently exogenous variable in such models. It is difficult to know to what extent this variable can be affected by conscious policy measures. Since South Africa accepted the GATT (WTO) principles in 1993, demand-side measures like direct producer subsidies, which worked by raising producer prices to compensate for the lack of competitiveness, are ruled out and what remains is, on the one hand, general economic policy measures and, on the other, supply-side interventions to stimulate exports by increasing competitiveness.

The macroeconomic framework to support exports is already in place. During the first half of 1996, the rand depreciated to the point where it was no longer overvalued, as was the case at the end of 1995, and perhaps even beyond that point, and the tight monetary policy has prevented a rapid real appreciation of the currency through increases in the domestic price level. In addition, as part of the GATT agreement, South Africa has undertaken to scrap quantitative import restrictions and reduce and unify tariffs, an undertaking that the country has fulfilled even faster than scheduled, and 'compensating' tariff reductions have been introduced in the government strategy to nullify the windfall gain made by exporters as a result of the rand depreciation – a gain which could otherwise erode the effort to reduce costs. This is fine, as far as it goes, but South Africa must also develop a comparative advantage in some manufacturing branches. This is not an easy task in an economy where the price system has been badly distorted in the past, to the point where it provided more or less completely useless information to producers about their inherent international strength or weakness.

Here is where the supply-side export promotion measures come into the picture. These measures include support in export marketing and schemes directed specifically at small and medium-sized firms, e.g. by facilitating credits, either generally, or specifically to enable them to meet export orders directly, and by subsidizing the employment of consultants for marketing or technology development. New measures include an accelerated depreciation scheme and a tax holiday for a maximum of six years.

To what extent supply-side measures will be effective is, however, very difficult to guess. Critics argue that measures have so far supported mainly larger firms and that there are hardly any schemes running which can be effectively approached by small businessmen.[64] Moreover, the incentives tend to pull in too many directions simultaneously, and it is not at all certain, for example, that tax holiday criteria with respect to location, labor intensity and 'priority industries' will stimulate exports. Once criteria get too vague or too contradictory the risk arises that everything, and hence nothing in particular, is supported, and this may be even more true for the export promotion program as a whole than for the individual sub-program. The money may be spread across too wide a spectrum of activities and too many and too diverging criteria may be used. Basically, the supply-side exercise is an exercise in finding areas where South Africa may have a comparative advantage, but then some concentration is needed. Picking winners *ex ante* is never easy, and supporting too wide a range of activities will not do the trick. Hence, we should not expect too many results to come out of the supply-side incentives.

The growth path envisaged by the *Growth, Employment and Redistribution* document could also be undermined by stabilization efforts. The way stabilization policy has been carried out in the past points to a possible tradeoff between growth and price stability. Monetary policy has been very tight during the past few years. This has, however, led to a situation where both nominal and real interest rates are so high that they tend to choke growth. It is not easy for companies to pay nominal rates of, say, 25 percent and remain competitive. Naturally, this in the past has put a heavy burden on companies to finance their investment out of their own profits and hence has also acted as a deterrent to growth. In the new strategy, increased tariff reductions are employed to put competitive pressure on South African companies and it is possible that this will contribute to containing inflation, but if this is not the case, restrictive monetary policy will remain the main instrument to combat inflation, whatever effects this may have on growth.

The tradeoff could come into play in different ways. One such way is through the skilled labor market. South Africa suffers from a severe lack of skilled labor. This constraint was one of the factors that put a brake on growth from about the mid–1970s,[65] and once growth gets going, this constraint may begin to operate again. The market for skilled labor will become increasingly tight and skilled wages will begin to increase which, in turn, may have 'contamination' effects on other parts of the labor market to the extent that agreements between employers and employees stipulate a certain relation between skilled wages and other wages. Thus, the wage-price spiral could be set in motion, the Reserve Bank would tighten monetary policy, the Department of Finance would have to follow suit and policy-induced recessionary tendencies would result.

Growth may also lead to a tightening of the monetary policy via the balance of payments. When GDP grows, in the South African case this results in increased imports. To the extent that the latter consist of producer goods or intermediate products used by the export industry, or import-competing branches, the deficit on the current account will only be temporary. However, since increased incomes tend to boost imports of consumer goods and inputs used by sectors producing non-tradables as well, the likelihood is high that monetary policy will be used to defend the rand to prevent inflationary pressures coming from the import side. Hence growth may be aborted before it becomes sustained.

Fiscal policy may choke growth as well. One of the pillars of the *Growth, Employment and Redistribution* strategy is its emphasis on prudent, re- strictive fiscal policy and a rapid reduction of the government budget deficit. This means that expenditures will have to be cut back quickly. Ideally, such cutbacks should be undertaken where they do least damage from the efficiency point of view. However, today South Africa is not in the position where this ideal can be met. The necessary administrative structures are not in place and, in addition, each department will tend to think that cuts should primarily take place elsewhere. In this situation, the likely outcome is that expenditure cuts will take place across the board, at more or less the same rate everywhere, and that productive public spending will be hurt as much as less productive.

The desire to cut the budget collides furthermore with the use of tax holidays to stimulate investment. A tight fiscal discipline will be difficult to maintain if the tax holiday policy becomes successful in the sense that many companies respond to it, since then fiscal revenue will be adversely affected. In fact, a tax arbitrage will be created which lends itself to all kinds of abuse. Thus it is, for example, difficult to avoid a situation where a company, once the tax holiday expires, creates subsidiaries that can be used *de facto* to prolong the period during which the company may take advantage of the incentives. This outcome lowers government revenue and hence, provided that the budget deficit is not allowed to grow, also government expenditure, and may thus jeopardize both growth and redistribution. The tax holiday may even delay a general lowering of the company tax rate, which, from the growth point of view, might perhaps be a better idea.

Another critical assumption is that flexibility in the labor market will generate employment and worker incomes and hence be an important weapon for combating poverty. The background to the emphasis on flexibility is to be found in a feeling that the recent growth increase in the economy has not resulted in employment creation to a corresponding extent[66] and without increased labor absorption it will not be possible to provide the projected 400,000 new jobs per annum in 2000. Flexibility could assume different forms, but presumably the most important one has to do with wages. Different sectors, regions and firms need different wage levels to be competitive. As could be expected, however, the unions are not in favor of flexibility, fearing that it will be expressed mainly in layoffs and reduced wages, so that as a condition for endorsing flexibility they will require something else in return.

This problem has been addressed by a presidential commission on labor market policy.[67] The solution advocated by this commission, and endorsed in the government strategy document as well, is one of a tripartite social accord involving employers, unions and government. The idea is that each of these three parties should put forward their own specific interest and opinions at the negotiating table; the unions would stress wages, the employers prices and investments and the government those expenditures on social programs and infrastructure that affect the welfare of the workers and enhance their productivity. Lower and more varied wages would be traded against price restraint, job-creating investment and different welfare measures. In this way, firms would gain competitiveness, workers a higher standard of living and government the freedom to embark on a more expansive course of economic policy without having to resort to tight monetary and fiscal policies to combat inflation.

Whether a social accord will ever be signed, however, remains doubtful, to say the least. This part of the strategy has a strong utopian flavor to it. The situation resembles the classical Prisoners' Dilemma. All the players could be better off by cooperating, but the incentives to break the accord, or never enter into it, are strong as far as both business and labor are concerned. Employers will face large difficulties when it comes to constitute themselves as a single, concerted player. In a market economy decisions with respect to prices and investment are made by individual firms and not on a central or regional level. Hence, a moral hazard problem will arise. Without adequate policing arrangements firms cannot be forced to maintain prices and make investments that are conducive to employment, and such policing arrangements do not exist in post-apartheid South Africa. That labor knows this will, in turn, foster a negative attitude in the unions. As long as the workers do not trust the employers to make credible commitments, they will not be prepared to show wage restraint.

Perhaps too much attention has already been paid to the question of how to bring about a social accord. It may not even be necessary. After the fall of apartheid South Africa has rejoined the international community which, in turn, means that we should expect the factor price equalization theorem to apply. With the gradual reduction of protection South African wages will increasingly resemble those prevailing elsewhere, i.e. they will tend to vary between sectors, and there may be little that domestic forces can do to change this tendency. There is, however, also considerable uncertainty with respect to what increased wage flexibility may actually achieve in terms of employment and income creation. Existing estimates of long-run employment elasticities are in the order of -0.7, i.e. a 10 percent wage reduction should lead to a 7 percent employment increase.[68] However, the methodology employed has been severely criticized in a recent ILO study[69] which also argues that growth in the recent past has been more employment-creating than conventional wisdom would lead us to believe. Actual wage flexibility could be higher than the available estimates indicate, not least in the informal labor market.

To what extent increased employment will succeed in alleviating poverty is also uncertain.[70] Income inequalities in South Africa are largely wage-driven. The overall contribution of wage inequality to overall income inequality in South Africa is 73.5 percent, but almost half the wage inequality is accounted for by the 34 percent of households with no wage income whatsoever, and 76 percent of those unemployed who belong to a household with no wage earner are poor. The latter figure declines, but not too drastically, when the number of wage earners in the family increases to one and two (53 and 57 percent, respectively; 56 and 66 for Africans, against 78; and 73 and 82, against 84, for rural households).[71] Thus, although there is no doubt that employment creation must be a central part of any development strategy in South Africa, mere access to employment does not automatically ensure poverty alleviation. Whether the latter can be achieved also depends on the size of the income generated. In addition, direct support measures to the poorest are necessary, especially in rural areas where employment is scarce *and* wage levels are particularly low.

## Conclusions

Economic policy-making in contemporary South Africa is not an enviable task. The government is under pressure from many quarters to deliver. The political promises made during the 1994 election campaign must be made good at some, not too distant, point in time. Of course, everybody cannot drive a Mercedes or have a swimming pool in the backyard, even in the long run, but a reasonable amount of employment must be created; and housing, education, health care and social programs must be provided to a reasonable extent. Otherwise, by definition, the transition to the 'after post-apartheid' stage will never be completed. The South African economy will remain a 'transitional' one for ever.

As we have demonstrated in the present chapter, there is no automatic mechanism that guarantees that the government will be able to honor its economic promises. Apartheid left a dismal heritage – one which it will be costly to get rid of. Even though, as we have pointed out, there are considerable efficiency gains to be had from moving away from the distorted situation that characterized the apartheid period, building the institutions, for example in the educational field, that make this possible will certainly require resources, but resources can only come out of economic growth. Now the ANC-led government has launched a macroeconomic strategy which is intended to make possible the realization of the *Reconstruction and Development Programme*. This strategy points both to a commitment to action and to a willingness to seek new ways when the old ones prove insufficient. Whether the new ways are the best ones available in the sense that they will deliver the desired results is, however, a completely different matter. To generate growth in South Africa is difficult, given that the government lacks control over some of the most critical components in the process. In order to succeed, the policy makers may need some luck too.

## Notes

1 Wilson and Ramphele (1989), McGrath (1983), (1990a), (1990b), McGrath and Whiteford (1994), Christopher (1994).
2 Hutt (1964), Lipton (1985), Lundahl, Fredriksson and Moritz (1992), Lundahl (1992), Moll (1990), (1993), Lewis (1990).
3 Lundahl and Ndlela (1980), Lundahl (1982).
4 Bunting (1969).
5 Wilson (1975), pp. 126–36.
6 van den Berghe (1967), Bunting (1969), de Klerk (1976).
7 Posel (1991).
8 Ibid., p. 5.
9 Ibid., p. 1.
10 Porter (1978), Lundahl (1982).
11 van Zyl Slabbert (1992), p. 20, cf. Lundahl (1989), Appendix.
12 Christopher (1994) pp. 32–35, Mbongwa, van den Brink and van Zyl (1996).
13 Nattrass (1981), pp. 119–23.
14 Hobart Houghton (1976), pp. 203–08, Reekie (1993).
15 Nattrass (1981), pp. 270–71.
16 Bell (1973).

17    Report of the Panel of Experts (1989).
18    Black, Siebrits and van Papendorp (1991).
19    van der Berg (1991), p. 80.
20    Iyengar and Porter (1990).
21    Little, Scitovsky and Scott (1970), Bhagwati (1978), Michaely, Papageorgiou and Choksi (1991).
22    Moll (1993), p. 11.
23    Levy (1992), p. 9.
24    Holden (1992), p. 320.
25    Moll (1989), pp. 146–47.
26    McCarthy (1988), p. 22.
27    Moll (1993), p. 11.
28    Holden (1992), p. 321.
29    van der Berg (1989), p. 37.
30    Wilson and Ramphele (1989), p. 18.
31    Whiteford and McGrath (1994), Whiteford, Posel and Kelatwang (1995), p. 21. It should be noted that the causes behind these figures differ slightly over time. It remains clear, however, that at all times inequalities between the races played a major role.
32    'At the beginning of 1994 the poverty line for an urban household with two adults and three children was approximately R840 per month, and R740 for a rural household with two adults and three children' (Whiteford, Posel and Kelatwang (1995), p. 2).
33    Whiteford, Posel and Kelatwang (1995), pp. 5, 8–9.
34    Wilson and Ramphele (1989), pp. 100–06.
35    Ibid., pp. 124–34.
36    Ibid., pp. 106–20.
37    Huddleston (1956), p. 160.
38    Spangenberg (1991), p. 18, Wilson and Ramphele (1989), pp. 138–49.
39    Nattrass (1992), p. 623.
40    Davies (1988), p. 173.
41    ANC Department of Economic Policy (1990).
42    Nattrass (1992).
43    Lundahl, Fredriksson and Moritz (1992), pp. 338–39.
44    Nattrass (1994).
45    ANC (1992).
46    MERG (1993).
47    Nattrass (1994).
48    ANC (1994).

49   *Business Day* (1995).

50   Ministry in the Office of the President (1996).

51   Naidoo (1995), p. 3.

52   Inter-Governmental Forum (1995).

53   South African Foundation (1996).

54   Social Equity and Job Creation (1996).

55   In addition, there were documents by Business South Africa (1996), the National African Federated Chamber of Commerce and Industry (1996), and the civic organizations (South African National Civic Organisation *et al.* (1996)). Most of the interest has, however, been concentrated to the views of established business interests and the unions, respectively.

56   Department of Finance (1996), p. 1.

57   Department of Finance (1996).

58   Ibid., p. 1.

59   Ibid., p. 5.

60   Ibid., p. 20.

61   This section has benefited substantially from conversations with Anthony Black, Murray Leibbrandt and Nicoli Nattrass, University of Cape Town, Keith Lockwood, South African Chamber of Business and Lieb Loots, University of the Western Cape, in July 1996. Nattrass (1996) and (forthcoming) Chapter 11, compare the government strategy with those proposed by the South African Foundation and the trade unions.

62   Growth, Employment and Redistribution (1996), p. 6.

63   Ibid., p. 7.

64   Interviews with Keith Lockwood, South African Chamber of Business, Johannesburg, 12 July, 1996, and Anthony Black, University of Cape Town, Cape Town, 17 July, 1996.

65   Lundahl, Fredriksson and Moritz (1992), pp. 312–17.

66   The output elasticity was 0.42, i.e. for every one percent increase of output, employment increased by 0.42 percent (Bhorat, Leibbrandt and Woolard (1995), p. 31).

67   Restructuring the South African Labour Market (1996).

68   Ibid., pp. 51–52.

69   Standing, Sender and Weeks (1996).

70   Bhorat and Leibbrandt (1996).

71   The higher figures for two-wage earner households are presumably due to the fact that no attempt was made to control for household size.

## References

ANC (African National Congress) Department of Economic Policy (1990), Discussion Document on Economic Policy. September. Johannesburg.

ANC (African National Congress) (1992), *Ready to Govern: ANC Policy Guidelines for a Democratic South Africa. Adopted at the National Conference 28–31 May 1992*. Policy Unit of the African National Congress. No place.

ANC (African National Congress) (1994), *The Reconstruction and Development Programme*. Umanyano Publications: Johannesburg.

Bell, Trevor (1973), *Industrial Decentralisation in South Africa*. Oxford University Press: Cape Town.

Bhagwati, Jagdish N. (1978), *Foreign Trade Regimes and Economic Development: Anatomy and Consequences of Exchange Control Regimes*. National Bureau of Economic Research: New York.

Bhorat, Haroon and Leibbrandt, Murray (1996), 'Understanding Unemployment: The Relationship between the Employed and the Jobless', in Baskin, Jeremy (ed.), *Against the Current: Labour and Economic Policy in South Africa*. Ravan Press: Johannesburg.

Bhorat, Haroon; Leibbrandt, Murray and Woolard, Ingrid (1995), 'Towards an Understanding of South Africa's Inequality', Paper delivered at the African Economic Research Consortium's Conference: Transitional and Long-Term Development Issues, Johannesburg, 30 November – 1 December.

Black, P.A., Siebrits, F.K. and van Papendorp, D.H. (1991), 'Homeland Multipliers and the Decentralisation Policy', *South African Journal of Economics*, Vol. 59.

Bunting, Brian (1969), *The Rise of the South African Reich*. Penguin Books: Harmondsworth.

*Business Day* (1995), 'Structural Flows Delay RDP', 9 June.

Business South Africa (1996), *Background Document for the 'Social Accord' Process*. Johannesburg.

Christopher, A. S. (1994), *The Atlas of Apartheid*. Routledge: London and New York.

Davies, Rob (1988), 'Nationalisation, Socialisation and the Freedom Charter', in Suckling, John and White, Landeg (eds.), *After Apartheid: Renewal of the South African Economy*. James Currey: London.

de Klerk, Willem A. (1976), *The Puritans in Africa: A History of Afrikanerdom*. Penguin Books: Harmondsworth.

Department of Finance (1996), *Growth, Employment and Redistribution*. Pretoria

'The Freedom Charter' (1988), in Suckling, John and White, Landeg (eds.), *After Apartheid: Renewal of the South African Economy*. James Currey: London.

Hobart Houghton, Desmond (1976), *The South African Economy*. Fourth edition. Oxford University Press: Cape Town.

Holden, Merle (1992), 'Trade Policy, Income Distribution, and Growth', in Schrire, Robert (ed.), *Wealth or Poverty? Critical Choices for South Africa*. Oxford University Press: Cape Town.

Huddleston, Trevor (1956), *Naught for Your Comfort*. Hardingham and Donaldson: Johannesburg.

Hutt, William H. (1964), *The Economics of the Colour Bar*. André Deutsch: London.

Inter-Governmental Forum (1995), *Toward a National Strategic Vision*. 27th November. No place.

Iyengar, Murali and Porter, Richard C. (1990), 'South Africa without Apartheid: Estimates from General Equilibrium Simulations', *Journal of International Development*, Vol. 4.

Levy, Brian (1992), 'How Can South African Manufacturing Efficiently Create Employment? An Analysis of the Impact of Trade and Industrial Policy'. Informal Discussion Papers on the Aspects of the Economy of South Africa. Paper No 1, South Africa Department, World Bank: Washington, D.C.

Lewis, Stephen R., Jr. (1990), *The Economics of Apartheid*. Council on Foreign Relations: New York and London.

Lipton, Merle (1985), *Capitalism and Apartheid. South Africa, 1910-84*. Gower: Aldershot.

Little, Ian; Scitovsky, Tibor and Scott, Maurice (1970), *Industry and Trade in Some Developing Countries. A Comparative Study*. Oxford University Press: London.

Lundahl, Mats (1982), 'The Rationale of Apartheid', *American Economic Review*, Vol. 72.

Lundahl, Mats (1989), 'Apartheid: *Cui Bono?*', *World Development*, Vol. 17.

Lundahl, Mats (1992), *Apartheid in Theory and Practice: An Economic Analysis*. Westview Press: Boulder, CO.

Lundahl, Mats; Fredriksson, Per and Moritz, Lena (1992), 'South Africa 1990: Pressure for Change', in Lundahl, Mats, *Apartheid in Theory and Practice: An Economic Analysis*. Westview Press: Boulder, CO.

Lundahl, Mats and Ndlela, Daniel B. (1980), 'Land Alienation, Dualism, and Economic Discrimination: South Africa and Rhodesia', *Economy and History*, Vol. 23.

McCarthy, Colin L. (1988), 'Structural Development of South African Manufacturing Industry', *South African Journal of Economics*, Vol. 56.

McGrath, Michael D. (1983), 'The Distribution of Personal Income in South Africa in Selected Years over the Period 1945 to 1980'. Ph.D. thesis. University of Natal: Durban.

McGrath, Michael D. (1990a), 'Income Redistribution: the Economic Challenge of the 1990s', in Schrire, Robert A. (ed.), *Critical Choices for South Africa: An Agenda for the 1990s*. Oxford University Press: Cape Town.

McGrath, Michael D. (1990b), 'Economic Growth, Income Distribution and Social Change', in Nattrass, Nicoli and Ardington, Elisabeth (eds.), *The Political Economy of South Africa*. Oxford University Press: Cape Town.

McGrath, Michael and Whiteford, Andrew (1994), 'Inequality in the Size Distribution of Income in South Africa', Stellenbosch Economic Project, Occasional Papers, No 10, Centre for Contextual Hermeneutics, University of Stellenbosch: Stellenbosch.

Mbongwa, Masiphula; van den Brink, Rozier and van Zyl, Johan (1996), 'Evolution of the Agrarian Structure in South Africa', in van Zyl, Johan, Kirsten, Johann and Binswanger, Hans P. (eds.), *Agricultural Land Reform in South Africa: Policies, Markets and Mechanisms*. Oxford University Press: Cape Town.

MERG (Macroeconomic Research Group) (1993), *Making Democracy Work: A Framework for Macroeconomic Policy in South Africa*. Centre for Development Studies, University of the Western Cape: Bellville.

Michaely, Michael; Papageorgiou, Demetris and Choksi, Armeane M. (1994), *Liberalizing Foreign Trade: Lessons of Experience in the Developing World*. Basil Blackwell: Cambridge, MA and Oxford.

Ministry in the Office of the President (1996), *Towards a National Infrastructure Investment Framework*. Second draft, 25 March. No place.

Moll, Terence C. (1989), '"Probably the Best Laager in the World": The Record and Prospects of the South African Economy', in Brewer, John D. (ed.), *Can South Africa Survive? Five Minutes to Midnight*. Macmillan: Houndmills, Basingstoke and London.

Moll, Terence (1990), 'Output and Productivity Trends in South Africa: Apartheid and Economic Growth'. Ph.D. thesis, Cambridge University.

Moll, Terence (1993), 'Once a Dog, Always a Dog? The Economic Performance of Modern South Africa', Paper prepared for ESM Research Conference '94, RAU, Johannesburg, 28-29 November.

Naidoo, Jay (1995), *Taking the RDP Forward.* Ministry in the Office of the President: Pretoria.

National African Federated Chamber of Commerce and Industry (1996), *Growth and Development with Equity Strategy.* Marshalltown.

Nattrass, Jill (1981), *The South African Economy: Its Growth and Change.* Oxford University Press: Cape Town.

Nattrass Nicoli (1992), 'The ANC's Economic Policy: A Critical Perspective', in Schrire, Robert (ed.) *Wealth or Poverty? Critical Choices for South Africa.* Oxford University Press: Cape Town.

Nattrass, Nicoli (1994), 'South Africa: The Economic Restructuring Agenda - A Critique of the MERG Report', *Third World Quarterly*, Vol. 5.

Nattrass, Nicoli (1996), 'Gambling on Investment, Growth and Equity: Competing Economic Visions in South Africa', Department of Economics, University of Cape Town: Cape Town.

Nattrass, Nicoli (forthcoming), *Intermediate Economic Theory*, Second edition. School of Economics, University of Cape Town: Cape Town.

Porter, Richard C. (1978), 'A Model of the Southern-African-Type Economy', *American Economic Review*, Vol. 68.

Posel, Deborah (1991), *The Making of Apartheid 1948-1961: Conflict and Compromise.* Clarendon Press: Oxford.

Reekie, W. Duncan (1993), 'Should South African Parastatals Be Privatised?', in Lipton, Merle and Simpkins, Charles (eds.) *State and Market in Post-Apartheid South Africa.* Witwatersrand University Press: Johannesburg.

*Report of the Panel of Experts on the Evaluation of the Regional Industrial Development Programme as an Element of the Regional Policy in Southern Africa* (1989). Development Bank of Southern Africa: Halfway House.

*Restructuring the South African Labour Market* (1996), Report of the Commission to Investigate the Development of a Comprehensive Labour Market Policy. CTP Book Printers: Cape Town.

*Social Equity and Job Creation. The Key to a Stable Future. Proposals by the South African Labour Movement* (1996). Issued by the Labour Caucus at Nedlac, incorporating Cosatu, Nactu and Fedsal: No place.

South African Foundation (1996), *Growth for All: An Economic Strategy for South Africa.* Johannesburg.

South African National Civic Organisation SANCO), South African Federal Council for the Disabled (SAFCD), Women's National Coalition (WNC) and National Rural Development Forum (NRDF) (1996), *Return to the RDP*. No place.

Spangenberg, J.P. (1991), *A Comparative Education Profile of the Population Groups in South Africa*. Development Bank of Southern Africa: Halfway House.

Standing, Guy; Sender, John and Weeks, John (1996), *Restructing the Labour Market: The South African Challenge*. ILO: Geneva.

van den Berghe, Pierre L. (1967), *Race and Racism: A Comparative Perspective*. John Wiley & Sons: New York.

van der Berg, Servaas (1989), 'An Interracial Income Distribution in South Africa to the End of the Century', *South African Journal of Economics*, Vol. 57.

van der Berg, Servaas (1991), 'Redirecting Government Expenditure', in Moll, Peter; Nattrass, Nicoli and Loots, Lieb (eds.), *Redistribution: How Can It Work in South Africa?* David Philip: Cape Town.

van Zyl Slabbert, Frederik (1992), *The Quest for Democracy: South Africa in Transition*. Penguin Books: London.

Whiteford, Andrew and McGrath, Michael (1994), *The Distribution of Income in South Africa*. Human Sciences Research Council: Pretoria.

Whiteford, Andrew; Posel, Dori and Kelatwang, Teresa (1995), *A Profile of Poverty, Inequality and Human Development*. Human Sciences Research Council: Pretoria.

Wilson, Francis (1975), 'Farming, 1866-1966', in Wilson, Monica and Thompson, Leonard (eds.), *The Oxford History of South Africa. II. South Africa 1879-1966*. Clarendon Press: Oxford.

Wilson, Francis and Ramphele, Mamphela (1989), *Uprooting Poverty: The South African Challenge*. W.W. Norton & Company: New York and London.

# 5 The South African economy in 1996: From Reconstruction and Development to Growth, Employment and Redistribution*

South Africa has come a long way since February 1990, when the ban on the ANC and other African political organizations was lifted and Nelson Mandela and other political prisoners were released from jail. Against heavy odds and after protracted negotiations in an atmosphere contaminated by periodic violence the political transition has been successfully completed. An interim constitution was adopted in November 1993 and the country saw its first free and democratic elections in April 1994. In May of that year the new president was sworn in and subsequently the Government of National Unity, constituted by all the major parties, began its work.

This situation lasted until April 1996. Once the text of the final constitution was in place,[1] the National Party left the governing coalition to go into opposition. What is left is a *de facto* ANC cabinet, and it is presumably only a matter of time before the Inkatha ministers will resign as well. The 1999 elections are drawing ever closer, and the coalition partners have started positioning themselves for that event.

In the meantime we may conclude that the political process has worked better than expected. The National Party did not enter the negotiations willingly, but the transition process was what Samuel Huntington has termed a transition by transplacement:

The label of *transplacement* is applicable 'when democratisation resulted largely from joint action by government and opposition groups'. Transplacement occurs when the reformers in the government gain the upper hand over the hardliners (those opposed to any change) and the government becomes willing to consider change, but is unwilling to independently initiate a change of regime. According to Samuel Huntington, this means that the government 'has to be pushed and/or pulled into formal or informal negotiations with the opposition. Within the opposition democratic moderates are strong enough to prevail over anti-democratic radicals, but they are not strong enough to overthrow the government. Hence they too see virtues in negotiation'.[2]

The initiative for the negotiations came from the ANC. Moreover, the Nationalists lost control over the negotiation process. From the second half of 1992, the ANC gradually defined the agenda and the eventual outcome bore a strong ANC imprint. Still, the negotiations constituted a positive-sum game, with gains for both parties. 'Both camps had turned to negotiation as a reluctant "second best" because there seemed to be no alternative, rather than from a desire for a historic reconciliation.'[3] It would have been impossible for the Nationalists to revert to Verwoerd-style apartheid.[4] In the words of Robert Schrire, they had to 'adapt or die'.[5] For the ANC armed struggle was an impossible option once international support for it was lost after the demise of communism in the Soviet Union and 'there was little chance that the opposition, even if it could combine its forces under the umbrella of a united Patriotic Front, would dethrone the government.'[6] Thus, the revolution that the more militant factions of the ANC had perhaps hoped would materialize became a 'negotiated revolution'[7] and Nationalist power gradually eroded during the negotiation process.[8] Compromise became the most important ingredient in the negotiations and in the Government of National Unity a consensual style of decision making developed, increasingly dominated, however, by the ANC.

Today, the Government of National Unity no longer exists. The ANC is alone, with the Nationalists in opposition, to be joined by Inkatha at any time between now and the 1999 elections. During the few months that have elapsed since the break-up of unity, not much opposition has been forthcoming from Nationalist quarters, naturally enough, because much of what the ANC government does is an outcome of past decisions endorsed by the Nationalists as well. After the resignation of the Nationalists from government, a new macroeconomic strategy, masterminded by the now ANC-led Department of Finance, has emerged,[9] and a presidential commission has delivered a report on labor market policy.[10] These documents and a few others issued by different interest groups before them[11] have added fuel to the economic policy debate – however, as we will see, hardly along party lines. Instead it seems as if the main division may be within the ranks of the ANC itself – notably between the government and the trade unions.

In the present chapter we will deal with developments in the South African economy since the beginning of the upturn in May 1993, when the longest recession that the country had experienced since World War II finally came to an end, with special emphasis on what has happened since the 1994 elections and the beginning of the Government of National Unity. We will begin with a sketch of the main macroeconomic trends and problems and move on to the implementation of the *Reconstruction and Development Programme* and the events that led to the formulation of the *Growth, Employment and Redistribution* strategy. Thereafter we will discuss the contents of this strategy in some detail as well as some of the main recommendations of the report of the presidential committee on labor market policy, which was delivered shortly afterwards and which is intimately related to the new macroeconomic strategy.

## GDP developments since 1993

The month of May 1993 constituted a turning point for the South African economy. The growth rate began to decline in the 1970s and during the 1980s the situation grew worse, with real GDP growing at an average rate that did not suffice to prevent per capita income from declining.[12] South Africa had entered a crisis that would not end until 1993. The years 1990, 1991 and 1992 all saw economic decline,[13] but from May 1993, output figures began to pick up. The recovery, however, turned out to be uneven. While the second half of 1993 witnessed and annualized growth rate of close to 6 percent, GDP *fell* at a rate of 1 percent during the first six months of 1994, increased again with 5.5 percent during the last half of the year and fell back to 1 percent in the first half of 1995. The average rate for these eight quarters was 3 percent,[14] and developments through the first quarter of 1996 were good enough to sustain this average – slightly more than the rate of growth of the population – using the second quarter of 1993 as the starting point.[15]

The uneven growth had several causes. Overall, the upswing has been broadly based, with strong growth especially in the secondary and tertiary sectors, with setbacks stemming largely from agriculture and mining. Demand began to recover during the first half of 1993, with consumer demand, however, remaining fragile in the face of job and wage uncertainty.[16] The first half of 1994 was a period of political uncertainty connected with the political transition, while the following six months saw an upswing because the process turned out to be an orderly one.[17] As a result, private domestic demand picked up, while at the same time public spending had increased in connection with the elections and the political transition.[18] The reduction during the first half of 1995 was mainly due to the impact of adverse weather conditions on agricultural output and frequent disruptions of work in the gold mines in combination with the higher costs associated with having to mine lower-grade ores.[19] Poor weather persisted throughout most of the year and it was not until the first quarter of 1996 that conditions improved in the agricultural sector. At the same time, the international demand for diamonds, base metals, and minerals increased but the effects of this were by and large offset by lower gold production.[20]

Private consumption responded to improved conditions more slowly than during previous recoveries (1977, 1983 and 1986). This was due to both economic and political factors. Employment and disposable income have grown relatively slowly and South African households have been reluctant to committing their future income to consumption in a political situation that they have interpreted as uncertain. The share of direct taxes in private income increased sharply, but the government exercised restraint in consumption expenditure which in turn contributed to the reduction of government dissaving.[21]

Real domestic fixed investment, on the other hand, after a sluggish start, gained enough momentum during 1994 to end up at a higher average than during the three preceding cyclical upswings: 8.5 percent during the first eight quarters.[22] Thereafter, the performance has been more uneven, with a slackening during the rest of 1995 and renewed acceleration in early 1996.[23] Much of the increased investment – which took place in virtually all sectors – came from replacement of obsolete equipment, notably transport equipment – a result of the prolonged recession and the considerable uncertainty surrounding political events since the mid-1980s.[24] During the second quarter of 1995, fixed gross capital formation had reached a share of 17 percent of GDP, against 15 percent when the upswing began in 1993.[25] This, however, fell short of the 25 percent deemed necessary of the economy were to absorb the yearly increase in the labor force. The net addition to the capital stock was no more than 3 percent of GDP, which, however was three times as much as during the low point during the first quarter of 1993, before the recovery had set in.[26]

Private domestic investment growth slackened somewhat at the beginning of 1996, but this slackening was more apparent than real. The reason was that by then the large mineral processing projects begun in 1993 and 1994, fueled by tax incentives in the form of accelerated depreciation allowances, had to a large extend been completed. If this is disregarded, increased private capital formation increased across a wide spectrum of sectors, with manufacturing in particular showing an upward trend from an already high level in 1995,[27] when net fixed investment in the sector increased by almost 50 percent. Also, investment in agriculture has increased as a result of expectations of increased future profit levels.[28] Public corporations have also contributed to the increase in capital formation, while the outlays of public authorities continued their downward trend until 1995, when spending on the *Reconstruction and Development Programme* began to have an impact.

As we will see later, domestic capital formation in South Africa has not yet increased to the level required for sustained growth of GDP at a rate which is high enough to provide for sustained increases of employment and real incomes as well. Nor has foreign investment been very helpful so far. The net inflow of capital not related to reserves has been positive since the latter half of 1994 but the depreciation of the rand and the general uncertainty surrounding the foreign exchange market during the first half of 1996 reduced this inflow to a mere trickle during the first quarter and, as it seems, led to a net outflow, mainly of short-term capital, in April and May.[29] The international financial markets continue to be quite sensitive to anything that is perceived as an indicator of economic, political, or social uncertainty.

**Sectoral developments**

Due to highly variable weather conditions, the contribution of agriculture to growth has varied considerably from year to year. 1993 was favorable and the second half saw an increase which amounted to no less than 29 percent on an annual basis. The following year was blessed with the second-largest maize harvest that South Africa has ever experienced. This was the main cause of a 12 percent growth of output in the sector. Thereafter, however, a severe drought set in which caused a reduction of the area devoted to maize of no less than one-quarter during the following growing season. This, together with increased imports which put downward pressure on profits in agriculture, made output contract by 15 percent in 1995. During the first quarter of 1996 weather conditions improved again and the sector re-covered.[30]

Agriculture has not been the only part of the primary sector that has experienced periodic problems since the beginning of the overall economic recovery in 1993. Gold mining has also been in trouble. South Africa's share of the world production of gold dropped from two-thirds in 1981 to 24 percent in 1993. This was due mainly to the expansion of output in the United States, Australia and Canada. At the same time, however, the quality of the ore mined declined.[31] During that year and the first half of 1995, both the quantity and the quality of the ore extracted declined. Quantity losses were caused by labor problems, a problem shared by the diamond mines as well, and the need to move into ores with lower and lower Ricardian rents increased costs and narrowed the margin between these and the prices obtained in international markets. The decline was large enough to outweigh the beneficial effects of increased international demand and increased productivity on the output of coal and some base metals. As a result, during the first two years of the upswing, the net contribution of mining to growth was minus 4 percent on average.[32] During the first quarter of 1996, the demand for diamonds, base metals, and minerals made for a strong increase in the value added of these products, but since gold production continued to have problems with low-yielding ores and high costs, the net result was a barely noticeable real increase for the sector as a whole: a mere 0.5 percent.[33]

Once we move to the secondary sector, the picture is brighter. It is here – in manufacturing – that we find the major forces behind the recovery. Output increased on a broad front, spurred by international demand stimulated by improved economic conditions in the industrialized nations at the same time as apartheid was being scrapped and the international relations of South Africa improved notably, by increased domestic demand, both for consumer and investment goods, and by the building of the Columbus stainless steel plant which began to produce in mid-1994. This produced a rate of growth that (together with that of transportation and communication) was higher than in any sector from the second quarter of 1993 to the second quarter of 1995: 4.5 percent per annum.[34] From the last quarter of that year, however, the rate of growth appears to have declined (it was even negative during the last three months of 1995), but this may be due to such factors as the reduction of delivery backlogs during the preceding three high-growth quarters. At any rate, the demand pattern appeared to be stable.[35]

The contribution of construction was far more modest, with an annual growth rate of only 1.5 percent until the second quarter of 1995, not least because the sector experienced a slower start, with no growth until 1994. As it seems, however, the trend is an upward one, spurred by an increasing demand for housing. Electricity, gas, and water, with an average growth rate of 3.5 percent over the same period, were off to a quick start as a result of an expansion program for electricity and could benefit from the overall improvement of the economy which called for more of these services.[36]

The tertiary sector grew at an average rate of 2.5 percent per annum until the second quarter of 1995, and at 4.5 percent during the rest of that year, but fell back to 0.5 percent at the beginning of 1996. As services are a highly diversified sector, it comes as no surprise that growth rates differed substantially among subsectors, with the highest rate obtained in transport and communication: 4.5 percent per annum on average up to the second quarter of 1995, closely followed by financial services and commerce, both with 3.5 percent. Households replaced their cars, the car rental business expanded, exports of automotive components increased and a cellular phone network was established in the country. Increased consumption of goods required increased transportation. Both retail and wholesale commerce expanded for the same reason. Financial services, finally, which had done relatively well during the recession, continued to increase their real value added as the securities and derivatives markets grew and from the generally sound financial conditions prevailing in the country.[37] The first quarter of 1996 saw a marked slowdown of tertiary growth: to no more than 0.5 percent, mainly as a result of a decline in retail commerce and a slowdown in transport and communication, while financial services did slightly better than in late 1995.[38]

## Employment, wages, income distribution and poverty

According to official figures, employment has not expanded *pari passu* with output during any of the economic recoveries since the 1970s. Non-agricultural formal employment continued to fall also after the economy had reached the turning point in 1993 and it was not until the following year that a slow increase began, with 0.6 percent on an annual basis, an increase that was, however, halted and converted into a decrease during the first half of 1995, a marginal increase during the third quarter of that year and a vigorous 3 percent growth during the last three months – as a result of increased hiring by public authorities, while private employment, which had increased during the first six months of 1995, contracted during the rest of the year.[39]

Employment remains the number one problem of the South African economy. During the 1989–93 recession an estimated 420,000 jobs were lost and at the end of 1994 the private sector had lost another 41,000 jobs.[40] Official figures indicate that during the latter half of 1994 and the entire year of 1995 the total number of unemployed had increased by 280,000.[41] The exact extent of unemployment is, however, a hotly debated issue. A 1993 survey conducted by SALDRU (South African Labour and Development Research Unit) reported a rate of 30.1 percent, a figure that was largely confirmed by the household survey carried out by the Central Statistical Service in October 1994: 32.6 percent, or 4.7 million people.[42]

These figures have, however, been questioned in a recent ILO report on the South African labor market.[43] They have been arrived at with the aid of the 'expanded' definition, according to which an unemployed person has to be 15 years or older, not in paid employment or self-employment, but available for such employment during the seven days preceding the interview, has taken specific steps during the four weeks preceding the interview to find employment *or* has the desire to take up employment. The alternative is to use a 'strict' definition of unemployment, one which contains all these criteria except the last. Thus, the difference between the two definitions is that the expanded one includes what is commonly known as 'discouraged workers', i.e. people who do not actively look for jobs but who would be prepared to work if the opportunity presents itself.[44] Excluding these workers by employing the strict definition yields far lower unemployment figures: 12.8 percent in the SALDRU survey and 20.3 percent in the 1994 case.[45] The latter is the figure deemed reasonable by the ILO team which argues that the strict definition is the one that best corresponds to how unemployment is being measured in other countries and in addition claims that due to a number of technical deficiencies,

available official statistics seriously underestimate the level of employment. Among those is the pervasive distrust factor on the part of the Censuses and surveys, which has hindered the accurate reporting of economic activity, the neglect of mining hostels in the October Household Survey (OHS), the inadequate sampling of the widely used World Bank-SALDRU survey of 1993, the omission of small-scale 'informal' units in the CSS employment series, the obsolescent sampling frame used in the industrial surveys, the poor coverage of illegal immigrant workers, and the major inconsistencies between the regular CSS series and the OHS for construction, public utilities and retail trade.[46]

According to this reasoning both measures overestimate unemployment, but the ILO team maintains that 20 percent is a reasonable 'guesstimate'.

On one level, it does not matter very much which of the two definitions one prefers; even 20 percent is a high rate of unemployment, and the ILO team admits this.[47] Employment still has to be one of the central objectives of government policy in South Africa. On another level, however, the question arises of how large the group of discouraged workers is. Two-thirds of the job seekers have been looking for employment for more than 12 months, and this is presumably a period which is long enough to have discouraged large numbers of potential workers from having searched for employment during the last four weeks – the requirement stipulated by the 'strict' definition.

There are good reasons for concentrating on the 'expanded' definition if the purpose is to get an idea of how serious the unemployment problem is in South Africa, especially since good social safety networks are often lacking. Over 70 percent of those who are unemployed have access to some income within the households of which they form part, but almost two-thirds of them belong to households below the poverty line.[48] Also, the ILO team does not provide any discussion of how it arrives at the 20 percent guess-timate.[49]

Once unemployment statistics are disaggregated by race, sex, age, and location, the preponderance of Africans, women, youths, and rural residents among the unemployed stands out. With the 'extended' definition, according to the 1994 data, unemployment amounted to 41.1 percent among Africans, 23.3 percent among Coloreds, 17.1 percent among Asians and 6.4 percent among whites. No less than 70 percent of the Africans had been looking for a job for more than a full year, against 56.2, 52.3, and 39.3 percent for the other three groups, respectively. Also, females were much worse off than men: 40.6 percent against 26.2, with one-half of the African women being jobless. The age group most hurt according to the SALDRU figures in the one between 16 and 24 years of age, with an average of no less than 53 percent unemployed, 64.8 percent among Africans and 71.2 percent among females belonging to that age cohort. Finally, according to the same source, unemployment hits rural areas much harder than urban ones: 40 percent against 25.7 (21.5 for Cape Town, Durban, and Johannesburg), with rural Africans reaching a rate of 41.8 percent.[50] Thus rural, young African women constitute the group with the lowest probability of formal employment in South Africa.

The employment problem is intimately related to the distribution problem. The total income of a South African household can be divided into the following six components (all of which do of course not have to be present): (1) remittances, (2) wage income, (3) income from agriculture, (4) capital income, (5) state transfers, and (6) income from self employment.[51] Wage income is the dominating category here, accounting for 69 percent of total income, followed by capital income (13 percent), with the remaining categories ranging between 3 and 6 percent.[52] Wage differences also dominate when it comes to the contribution to total inequality. No less than 73.5 percent of the latter is caused by wage inequality. This figure, however, should be interpreted with some caution, because 34 percent of all households have no access to wage income at all, and these households account for 46 percent of the wage inequalities.[53] What this means is that employment creation is potentially very important from the distributional point of view. We will come back to this below.

Unemployment is also one of the most important determinants of poverty. No less than 53.3 percent of all unemployed belong to households with no wage earner. Of those unemployed no less than 76.1 percent are poor and 36.1 percent live in deep poverty (half the income of the poverty line). A further 32.7 percent of the unemployed are members of households with a single wage earner, 53 percent of them are poor, and 19.1 percent are in deep poverty. Thus, as many as 86 percent of the unemployed are members of households with either no or a single wage earner and the majority of them are poor (67.3 percent), and almost one-third (29.6 percent) are in deep poverty.[54]

**Prices and wages**

Inflation had been persistently high for about two decades before it began to come down in 1992. In 1989 the Reserve Bank began to tighten monetary policy and defend the nominal value of the rand, but due to such factors as high oil prices in the wake of the Kuwait crisis, wage increases, and bad harvests it took a few years until the rate of inflation would start to come down.[55] The combination of a tight monetary policy and a drawn-out recession between 1989 and 1993, which affected both wage settlements and inflation expectations, supported by relative price stability among South

Africa's most important trading partners and a stabilization of the rand, resulted in marked reduction of the rate of increase of producer prices from late 1990 to October 1993 – from almost 15 percent to 5.4 – and in consumer prices from late 1991 to April 1994 – from 16.8 percent to 7.1, figures which in both cases had not been experienced since 1972.

Thereafter, however, the rate of inflation began to rise again, however, at a slower pace than during any of the previous upturn since 1972. In April 1995, the annual rate of increase of producer prices had accelerated to 11.5 percent and that of consumer prices to 11.0 percent. Initially, the main impacts came from the increase of food prices due to bad weather, but at the end of 1994 increases in labor costs took over as the main driving force behind producer price rises. Bad weather also had an influence on consumer prices, but in 1995 the impact of increased demand came as a result of the upturn and a sharp increase in import prices. Credits to households had increased and so had the broadly defined money supply. Finally, the deficit on the government budget, which we will come back to below, contributed to the price increases.[56]

In 1995, the rate of increase of both the producer and the consumer price index slowed, a trend which by and large persisted through the first three months of 1996. In April of the latter year, consumer price rises were down to 5.5 percent on an annual basis – the lowest rate since April 1972. The month before, producer price increases had fallen to 5.9 percent. There were several reasons behind these developments. Labor costs per unit of production grew at a slower pace, food prices increased more slowly, monetary policy remained conservative, tariffs were reduced on imported goods, and the exchange rate remained relatively stable until the depreciation of the rand in February 1996,[57] which was followed by a second depreciation in July. These exchange rate changes are likely to contribute to increased inflation in the future.

One of the main ingredients in the inflationary spiral in South Africa, as in other countries, has been the development of wages, or, rather, the labor cost per unit of output. Nominal wage and salary increases (outside agriculture) were quite high at the end of the 1980s and the beginning of the present decade, 18.4 percent in 1989 and 15.2 percent in 1992. It was not until the following year that a cut to 10.5 percent could be achieved,[58] and after a temporary increase to 12.0 percent in 1994, the average rise in 1995 could be kept down to 9.6 percent.[59]

The increases in wages and salaries must be compared to the increases in real output per worker that took place during the same period. Outside agriculture, these rose from 0.4 percent in 1991 to 2.8 percent in 1993 and 1994 and 3.2 percent in 1995. Thus, the growth of nominal labor costs per unit of output slowed from 17.3 percent in 1990 to 7.4 percent in 1993, to rise again to 9.1 percent the following year and fall back to 6.2 percent in 1995. By the latter period a decline had been achieved in real terms: minus 2.1 percent.[60] Thus, from the point of view of investment and employment, the relation between wage and salary increases on the one hand and labor productivity increases on the other has improved, but it still remains to be seen whether this trend will be sustained over a longer period. The wage issue is a central one and will be discussed at some length below.

The monetary policy of the Reserve Bank has remained more or less tight since the beginning of the upswing in 1993. The rationale for this is spelled out by the bank as follows:

> The adoption of the objective to achieve price stability does not mean that the monetary authority believes that the problems of low economic growth, unemployment and wealth creation are unimportant. The need for high and sustained economic growth is fully recognised and supported by the South African Reserve Bank. However, the Bank is convinced that the best contribution it can make towards achieving sustainable economic growth and development is to create a stable financial environment.[61]

The Reserve Bank sets a target for the expansion of the money supply during a given year and attempts to keep interest rates positive in real terms, as a minimum. The bank carefully watches domestic credit growth, changes in foreign currency reserves and exchange rate changes. It was successful in bringing the rate of inflation down to levels that had not been experienced for over two decades during the first four months of 1994. However, as the growth of the money supply consistently exceeded the upper guideline limit of 9 percent, a number of steps were taken to tighten monetary policy. The bank rate (the rate at which the Reserve Bank makes loans to banking institutions) was increased in three steps until June 1995. Secondly, the guidelines for the monetary supply envisioned a low growth rate (6–10 percent) both in 1995 and 1996. These were complemented by conservative guidelines to banks with respect to the growth of credit in the private sector (10 percent), which had been growing at an increasing pace until reaching a figure of 19.5 percent in June 1995. Finally, minimum cash reserve requirements were raised. These measures brought the growth rates of both the broadly defined money supply and credit to the private sector down, but not enough to keep them within the targeted ranges, and in April 1996 the bank rate was again increased.[62]


**Foreign trade and the balance of payments**

South Africa's external relations, both on the trade side and the capital flow side, have undergone a fundamental change as a result of the political developments that led to the scrapping of apartheid and the first democratic elections. In 1995 nothing remained of the sanctions that had been imposed by the international finance community ten years earlier and South Africa had itself begun to turn its inward-looking trade policy around – a policy which had been inaugurated no less than seven decades before.

South Africa participated in the final stages of the Uruguay Round of trade negotiations in December 1993 and in April 1994 the country signed the Marrakesh Agreement establishing the World Trade Organization (WTO). This means that South Africa henceforth will have to comply with the statutes of the new organization.[63] The first steps in the direction of a more outward-looking trade regime had, however, been taken a few years before, in 1990, with the creation of the General Export Incentive Scheme (GEIS). This scheme subsidizes manufacturing exports directly, via a formula that is based on such variables as the export volume of the company, the degree of processing, the use of local inputs, and the effective exchange rate (the value of the rand in relation to a certain currency basket).[64] Since the GEIS scheme entails measures that are linked directly to export volumes it is in conflict with WTO statutes, and a decision has therefore been made to phase the scheme out at the end of 1997. The decision has also been founded on the inefficiency of the program, which provided supports for exports that were already viable on their own, discriminated against small firms, and encouraged rent-seeking and outright fraudulent practices, but 'seemed to have little effect on encouraging export-oriented investment'.[65]

The main ingredient in the new trade policy is the redressing of the anti-trade bias that characterized the import substitution policy that had been in place since the 1920s. The Marrakesh Agreement stipulated the abolition of quantitative import restrictions and other non-tariff barriers to trade and the new tariff policy which took effect in South Africa at the beginning of 1995 provides for a unification of tariff levels and a rapid reduction of tariffs until reaching the levels compatible with WTO statutes. Colin McCarthy summarizes what has so far been achieved:

> The tariff structure has been reduced from about 10,000 tariff lines to between 5,000 and 6,000 lines and the multitude of over 100 tariff levels reduced to six rates within a range between 0 and 30 per cent, the tariffs for clothing and motor vehicles excepted. The phased reduction of tariff levels by an average of one-third over five years commenced in early 1995, and in some sectors the progress is ahead of schedule. Remaining quantitative controls were replaced with *ad valorem* tariffs. The import surcharges were progressively lowered and eliminated in October 1995. The phasing out of GEIS towards its final termination by the end of 1997 has also advanced far, especially with drastic cuts in GEIS towards its final termination by the end of 1997 has also advanced far, especially with drastic cuts in GEIS payouts as from 1 July 1996.[66]

Thus, even though the anti-export bias has not been eliminated completely it has been reduced considerably in comparison with the situation in 1994.

Progress has also been made with respect to trade relations. By and large these have now been normalized. South Africa became a member of the Southern African Development Community (SADC) in August 1994. The country has also been granted the benefits included in the Generalized System of Preferences conceded by the European Union and a few other OECD countries, like the United States, Canada, Japan, and Norway.[67]

Some problems remain to be solved, however. Thus, the Southern African Customs Union (SACU) has to be renegotiated with Botswana, Lesotho, Namibia, and Swaziland. The smaller countries have shown dissatisfaction with respect to the size and timing of the payments that are intended to compensate these countries for higher prices as a consequence of the use of South African tariffs and quantitative import restrictions, loss of fiscal discretion, and polarization of economic development, with South Africa benefiting from industrialization and growth while the smaller states end up in a backwater.[68] South Africa has in turn argued that the revenue-sharing formula which gives the smaller countries more than what they should get if their respective shares in the union's imports had been used constitutes a burden on the South African fiscus which the country is not prepared to accept. A Customs Union Task Team (CUTT) was appointed to look into these and other issues towards the end of 1994 and make recommendations with respect to suitable changes of the customs union agreement. The CUTT was given five months to come up with a solution, but has not produced any report so far.[69]

South Africa also has to sort out its trade relations with the rest of the countries in southern and eastern Africa, but it has so far not decided to join the Common Market of Eastern and Southern Africa (COMESA), which was established in 1993, from the old PTA (Preferential Trade Area for Eastern and Southern African States), by the adoption of a goal of a common external tariff. This has caused some resentment on the part of COMESA, especially since South Africa is running huge trade surpluses with the other countries in the region.[70] Recently a bilateral trade agreement was concluded with Zimbabwe, but only after considerable friction. Zimbabwe wanted free access to the South African market especially for its clothing and textile products. However, when the bilateral preferential trade agreement between the two countries expired at the end of 1992 it was not renewed and subsequent negotiations for a long time led nowhere.[71] Both employers and employees in the South African textile sector opposed concessions to Zimbabwe and it was not until September 1996 that a new bilateral agreement went into effect.

International relations have been normalized also on the financial side. In 1985, the international banks decided to call in their loans to the country, which refused to do anything about apartheid. South Africa retaliated by declaring a partial standstill on repayments. With apartheid being a thing of the past, a final rescheduling of foreign debt was negotiated in 1994. South Africa has also come back as a borrower in the international capital markets and issued bonds for 750 million US dollars in December 1994 and 30 billion yen in May 1995.[72]

In the long run full financial liberalization in envisaged by the government. To that end, the financial rand was abolished in March 1995. The financial rand, which had been used for foreign investment and repatriation of capital, offered South African currency at a lower price in terms of foreign currency than the commercial rand used for other transactions, which made it easy to invest in the country but provided a disincentive to bringing profits out. Hence, it acted as an obstacle to foreign investment and was therefore abolished when it was felt that it was no longer needed for balance of payments reasons.[73] For South African citizens, exchange controls remain in place, however. Although a relaxation of these controls has been envisaged it is not clear when it may be effected.

The changed international standing of South Africa and the changes with respect to trade and exchange rate policy have had an impact on the balance of payments. Between 1985 and 1994, for nine and a half years, South Africa had experienced a large net capital outflow not related to its currency reserves: 51.7 billion rand. Traditionally, the country had been a net importer of capital, which in turn had meant that it did not have to worry about its current account. Once the foreign banks started to call in their loans in 1985, this changed and South Africa had to maintain a surplus on its current account instead. This situation acted as a brake on economic growth until the third quarter of 1994 when a net capital inflow again allowed the current account to show a deficit.[74]

This situation continued until February 1996, when the rand, which had been overvalued at the end of 1995, began to depreciate – with 16 percent in nominal terms until the end of April. As a result, the net inflow of capital virtually dried up during the first three months of 1996 and a net outflow is likely to have taken place in April and May. Both were caused by the sensitivity of short-term flows.[75] A second depreciation of the rand, in July, caused on the one hand by the termination of Reserve Bank intervention in the forward exchange market and on the other hand by a rumor that Chris Stals, the president of the bank and the personification of a conservative stance in monetary matters, was about to resign presumably had similar effects although no figures are available at the moment of writing.[76]

The deficit on the current account of the balance of payments, caused mainly by the general upswing in the economy, continued into the first quarter of 1996. The rise in domestic expenditure led to an increase in the value of merchandise imports of 27 percent in 1994 and a further 15 percent (on an annual basis) during the first half of 1995. The marginal import propensity is high in South Africa, with the value of imported goods increasing by 3.4 percent for each percentage point increase of real domestic expenditure (private and government consumption, fixed investment, and inventory accumulation) during the current upswing.[77] The most rapid increase in terms of volume was registered in capital goods, but intermediate products and consumer goods also displayed significant increases. The period also saw an increase in import prices, mainly as a result of the more or less continuous depreciation of the rand.[78]

Turning to the export side, the volume of net gold exports decreased by more than one-fourth from the second quarter of 1993 to the second quarter of 1995. This, was, however, compensated for by an increase in the rand price of gold through May 1996, so that the value of gold exports increased by about 2 percent from 1993 to 1994 but fell back slightly during 1996, to rise again at the beginning of 1996. Gold exports are strongly dependent on international price developments, since South Africa has reached a stage where increased export volumes require lower and lower grades of ore to be milled. This is not the only problem, and in the short run it has not even been the most serious one:

> The sharp drop in the volume of net gold exports in 1994 and the first half of 1995 ... could not only be attributed to a lowering in the quality of ore milled to preserve the life of the gold mines. A much more important cause of this decline was a sharp contraction in the throughput of ore because of the closure of some mines; poor labour productivity, reflecting labour disputes and an additional number of special and new holidays; technical difficulties owing to seismic incidents; and a serious mining accident in the first half of 1995.[79]

Viewed in a longer perspective, however, the gold mines of South Africa have to compete with mines in, for example Australia, Canada, and the United States where labor productivity is sometimes more than ten times the South African level and where South African wage levels are higher than those of its main competitors.[80] This, and not the short-run problems, is what is making it increasingly difficult for the gold mines to compensate in the export markets.

The value of South African non-gold exports, on the other hand, has shown a steady upward trend since mid-1993. However, prices of South Africa's export goods have increased far less than international commodity prices in general, partly because of the composition of international demand but also because some products are exported on a fixed-price contract basis. This, in turn, has made for a comparatively slower increase in volume, during 1994 and 1995.

Several factors contributed to the increased exports. The expansion of economic activity in industrial countries and the normalization of South Africa's international economic relations were accompanied by a depreciation of the rand and a change of trade policy which increased the incentives to export. The increase took place across all the main sectors, but the main impetus came from manufacturing, notably chemical products, machinery, transport equipment and paper products. At the beginning of 1996 it appeared as if manufacturing exports were leveling off at the 1995 level, both because some branches were experiencing capacity constraints and because there may have been a tendency to concentrate more on the expanding domestic market.[81]

The service and transfer account displayed a deficit during the recession years before 1993 and this deficit continued to grow until early 1996, with the exception of 1995. With the exception of tourism, service payments abroad increased in 1994 and 1995 and this was only partly offset by increased receipts, mainly from tourism. During 1996 dividend and interest payments from abroad contracted while at the same time South African tourists increased their spending abroad.[82]

The net result of rapidly increasing merchandise imports and an increasing deficit on services and transfers on the one hand and less rapidly growing exports on the other has been widening deficits both on the trade and on the current account, with the latter going from a surplus of 5.4 billion rand in 1993 to a deficit of 12.8 billion in 1995.[83] This was, however, covered by capital inflows, both long and short term, before short-term capital started to leave South Africa as a reaction to the turbulence in the foreign exchange market in 1996. The deficit on the capital account, which amounted to 15 billion rand in 1993, had by 1995 been converted into a surplus of 21.7 billion.[84]

The first inflows in 1994 and 1995 consisted mainly of short-term capital in the form of trade finance and revolving credit facilities, but as the credit ratings of South Africa improved abroad, the inflow of long-term capital picked up as well, during the second half of 1994. Subsequently, in December of the same year, the government successfully issued 2.7 billion rand's worth of bonds in the international capital market, to be followed by a Samurai bond issue of another 1.3 billion in May 1995. The private sector raised a total of 2.2 billion rand during the last quarter of 1994 and the first two of 1995. Non-residents also contributed to the long-term inflow by purchasing South African securities for 2.2 billion in 1994 and at an increasing pace after the abolition of the financial rand the following year until a figure of 4.7 billion was reached during the first quarter of 1996. What has, however, been missing from the picture is investment in direct equity capital by non-residents. Even though the confidence in South Africa has increased greatly abroad, it has not improved enough to trigger a large-scale inflow of direct investment.[85]

A consequence of the increased capital inflow has been that South Africa's foreign debt has increased from 25.5 billion US dollars at the end of 1993 to 27.9 billion at the end of 1994 (latest available figure) – 22.9 percent of GDP. However, the renegotiated debt, i.e. the part of the outstanding debt that had been subject to standstill since 1985, continued its decrease, from 4.4 billion in 1993 to 3.4 at the end of the following year.[86]

At the same time the overall balance of payments position of South Africa improved from mid-1994. The country's net gold and currency reserves increased by 15.4 billion rand from July 1994 to December 1995, to shrink again during the turbulent first quarter and April of 1996. At the end of June 1995 the gross reserves amounted to 15.2 billion rand which sufficed to cover six weeks' imports. At the end of May 1996, this figure had, however, declined to 11 billion, in the wake of the first currency depreciation of the year.[87] (Traditionally, the goal of the Reserve Bank has been three months' imports.)

**Government finances**

In the discussion of inflation it was pointed out that monetary policy has remained more or less tight during the present upswing in the economy. To this corresponds a fiscal policy with partly similar aims:

> The government is committed to pursuing policies which will lead to higher investment and employment and to sustainable economic growth within a framework of macroeconomic stability. The *prime objective* of fiscal policy in this broader context is to achieve fiscal sustainability in the medium term, including the reprioritisation of government expenditure so as to increase allocations for social services, capital expenditure and the Reconstruction and Development Programme. Equally important are the improved management of the public sector and the efficient use of available resources. The tax system is also undergoing a structural reform to enhance its efficiency and equity, while ensuring that the tax burden does not increase.[88]

We will come back to the expenditure part of the *Reconstruction and Development Programme* (RDP) below. Here we will concentrate on the other aspects. The most immediate concern of the South African government is to reduce the deficit in the government budget over a five-year period. In 1992/93 this deficit amounted to no less than 9 percent of GDP and the following fiscal year an even higher figure was registered: 9.8 percent. These levels clearly threatened to accelerate inflation and lead to a further tightening of an already tight monetary policy. The fiscal situation was unsustainable and the Government of National Unity hence set out to bring the deficit down. In 1994/95 the deficit had been reduced to 5.6

percent, the preliminary figure for 1995/96 is 6 percent and the budget figure for 1996/97 is 5.1 percent.[89] By 1998/99 it was intended that the deficit should be reduced to 4 percent of GDP.[90]

Since South Africa is a high-tax country viewed in an international perspective, there is little scope for closing the gap by increasing the tax burden, so the main thrust must come from a reduction of expenditure. In particular, government consumption should be cut. Otherwise the investment necessary of carrying out, for example, the RDP could easily be jeopardized. Also, wage and salary increases in the public sector have to be kept within the limits given by the rate of inflation.

Another way of reducing the budget deficit is by increasing the efficiency of tax administration and collection. To this end, a program has been launched to train revenue personnel in general and to improve customer service, and measures have been undertaken to combat tax evasion, including an amnesty to people not previously registering as taxpayers.[91]

Government revenue as a percentage of GDP has increased slightly since the beginning of the upswing, from 24.2 percent in 1992/93 to 25.2 percent in 1994/95 and an estimated 25.5 percent the following year, with 25.8 percent being budgeted for 1996/97.[92] This means that what is 'accepted as the ceiling on the tax revenue'[93] has been reached. Total expenditure has exceeded revenue over the entire period, but, as we have already found, the difference has narrowed somewhat over time.

Virtually all of the government revenue comes from taxes, with personal income and company tax revenue accounting for the largest share, followed by value-added and similar taxes. With the exception of taxes on property, these are also the categories that have contributed most to the increase of government revenue in recent years. The value-added tax rate was increased in 1993/94, a temporary transition levy on the income tax was introduced the following year, and excise duties were increased during both years. Increased efficiency in income tax collection has contributed as well. Expenditure has also been restructured, with comparatively more going to the social sectors and less to protection and the economic sectors.[94]

Finally, it should be mentioned that government debt has displayed an upward trend, from a low 37.2 percent of GDP at the end of the fiscal year 1990/91 to 55.1 percent at the end of 1994/95. There were several reasons for this, notably the large financing requirements of the new government (some of which we will come back to below), and the inclusion of the debt of the former homelands.[95] This left a gross borrowing requirement for 1996/97 of 45.1 billion rand.[96]

## The Reconstruction and Development Programme

For many years the ANC did not have any well-defined economic strategy. It was not until the 1994 elections became imminent that a reasonably coherent policy document was produced. This document was the *Reconstruction and Development Programme* (RDP), which was taken over in its entirety as the economic strategy of the Government of National Unity after the elections.[97] The RDP spelled out the economic and social agenda for the next five years, up to the 1999 elections. It attempts to integrate 'growth, development, reconstruction and redistribution into a unified programme'.[98]

The main pillars of the RDP are those of redistribution and satisfaction of basic needs. The document springs from a long discussion of how to redress the damage done by apartheid which began with the *Freedom Charter* resolution in 1955.[99] It is very concrete in its promises with respect to what the government is to deliver. Five key programs are identified: (1) meeting basic needs, (2) developing human resources, (3) building the economy, (4) democratizing the state and society, and (5) implementing the RDP. In the following section we will concentrate on the first two of these, the ones dealing with the more or less direct delivery of items that are directly related to the welfare of the citizens. The other aspects, with the exception of (4), which falls outside the scope of the present work, will be touched upon in the discussion of the subsequent fate of the program.

The list of basic needs is long. First in line is job creation. Here the government is given a 'leading' Keynesian role: providing employment for women and youths in poor rural areas. Second on the list is land reform. The 1913 and 1936 land acts drastically reduced the area to which the Africans were to have access and confined them to lands of lesser quality, and to reverse this discrimination the RDP envisages a land redistribution program that will operate on various levels, 'including strengthening property rights of communities already occupying land, combining market and non-market mechanisms to provide land, and using vacant government land'.[100] In particular, a land claims court has been set up to deal with cases of forced removals.

Third, South Africa has a tremendous backlog of housing for all racial groups except Whites and then in particular for Africans, both in urban and rural districts. 'At minimum', the RDP states, one million low-cost houses should be constructed over a five-year period to cover the needs of poor households.[101] Fourth, clean water and sanitation are needed by everybody. The aim is to provide 20–30 liters of clean and safe water per capita per day within 200 meters distance from the home in the short run as well as adequate and safe sanitation facilities, including refuse removal in urban areas. Fifth, 2.5 million new homes should be supplied with electricity by the year 2000.

Telecommunications also fall within the basic needs category according to the RDP, but the program is not very explicit when it comes to targets: 'The RDP aims to provide universal affordable access for all as rapidly as possible within a sustainable and viable telecommunications system ...'[102] Only schools and clinics are targeted, to be serviced within two years from the beginning of the program. In the transport sector emphasis is put on developing public transport in general and in rural areas in particular, but without any quantification of the goals. Environmental considerations include waste management, safe work places in terms of pollution, noise, and dangerous practices as well as environmental education at all levels. Malnutrition is a serious problem among the South African poor and the RDP states emphatically that 'as soon as possible, and certainly within three years, every person in South Africa ... [must] get their basic nutritional requirement each day and ... no longer live in fear of going hungry'.[103] This is envisaged to take place through employment creation, land reform, and the general reorganization of the economy. Health care is also a priority area, one where 'the complete transformation of the entire delivery system' is seen as necessary 'in order to redress the harmful effects of apartheid'.[104] To this end, a shift of emphasis must take place from curative hospital care to preventive primary health care in district health units. Children, aged, disabled, unemployed, and students are targeted for free health care, the first group immediately and the others within five years. Finally, the RDP envisages major reforms within the areas of social security and welfare, including pensions and social assistance in cash or in kind, but not in very concrete terms.

The second key program deals mainly with education, which could of course also have been included among the basic needs, but which is singled out for special treatment in the *Reconstruction and Development Programme*. Education is dealt with in fairly general and sweeping terms. The main objective is the reversal of the discrimination resulting from the apartheid system and the increased provision of education and training for girls and women. The most concrete goal is that of a 10-year compulsory education for everybody 'as soon as possible' in classes not exceeding 40 students at the turn of the century.[105]

A government white paper on reconstruction and development outlined the policies deemed necessary to carry the program out.[106] The RDP was to be financed mainly out of a special fund that had been constituted by reallocation of resources from the regular government departments. This fund amounted to 2.5 billion rand during the first fiscal year (1994/95) and was to increase gradually until reaching 12.5 billion in 1998/99. Foreign aid was to be sought, however, not in order to increase the RDP budget, but to obtain cheaper financing for the program. This was to be complemented with interest revenue on the fund, sales of state assets, and revenue from lotteries and gambling. Distorting tax increases were to be avoided and so were inflationary policies. Government expenditure was to be kept under control and the budget deficit should be narrowed over time. Government debt was not to increase as a result of the RDP. The prudent, conservative, monetary policy would not be changed.

The idea was to make sure that the RDP could be implemented with the normally available government revenue. The basic needs component of the program was coupled with a growth strategy, as it was clear that without growth the scope for redistribution would be severely circumscribed.[107] To this end the program envisaged a dynamic trade and industry policy which, complemented by educational measures to increase the stock of human capital, was to enhance the international competitiveness of South Africa and make the country an attractive one for international investors. Political stability and a consistent economic policy were also to contribute to the latter end.

The need for a new trade and industry policy stemmed from the realization that gold exports and exports of other minerals could no longer be relied upon to guarantee a high and sustained rate of growth in the economy. South Africa needed to have its exports, in those segments of the world market where the demand was high and increasing. Here, the state could step in with investments in infrastructure and with support to industries that could compete in the world market, branches that processed primary products for export and labor-intensive lines of production that would have a potentially beneficial effects on employment. In general, value added in manufacturing should be increased through a combination of education, development of technology and improved work organization.

Increased competitive pressure was seen as necessary to counteract monopolies and inefficient large companies. To this end anti-trust legislation was envisaged and tariffs were to be gradually reduced until reaching the level allowed by GATT. These squeeze measures would be complemented by supply-side measures like capacity building, training and education, as well as a better utilization of available technology. Small and medium-sized companies were targeted for special support.

## Accomplishments and problems

The *Reconstruction and Development Programme* was barely able to survive two years as government policy in its original form. Of the 2.5 billion rand budgeted for 1994/95, 1.7 billion had to be rolled over to 1995/96 and, as it seems, 20 percent or more of the budget for the following year will probably share the same fate.[108] The reason was simply that the administrative structure that was required for efficient spending was not yet in place. Local elections were yet to be held in South Africa, i.e. political leadership was lacking on the lower levels where much of the RDP had to be carried out.

A review of the program was presented by the RDP office in the Office of the President after the first year of operation.[109] In his inaugurational speech, President Mandela had promised that delivery of the RDP would start within 100 days of the new government. A special effort was therefore made to kickstart the program, via the identification of 22 so-called presidential lead programs, designed not only for rapid delivery but also with a view to building a learning process into the implementation. The review document stresses the importance of timing and monitoring: 'The RDP and its Fund works on the basis of clear goals, time frames and indicators that give feedback on performance.'[110] In spite of these ambitions it is difficult to get any idea of how much had actually been carried out during the first year. Little quantitative information is provided, which is after all only natural since many of the programs had been designed to be completed over several years.

At any rate, the land redistribution and restitution program had got underway with 6,750 families benefiting during the first year. The *Free Health Care Programme* had ensured that no children under the age of 6 and no pregnant women would be turned away from hospitals or clinics, four times as many patients than before were being treated in rural areas, and the number of hospital admissions of young children had dropped as a result of improvements in primary health care. A project for building and upgrading clinics was underway. 100 million rand had been allocated for school renovation, etc. during 1994/95, but no information is given with respect to how much had actually been spent.

The electrification program was ahead of target (easy enough, given the excess capacity of ESCOM, the electricity company). A program for the extension of municipal services had been started, but presumably not too much had been achieved, since this type of program depends heavily on local efforts, not least for funding. A public works program related to all the other lead programs had been launched. 5.4 million school children had been provided with a sandwich every morning, instead of having to go to school on an empty stomach. A small-scale farmer development program was in its very infancy, and this was the case also with an urban renewal program. Pilot projects had been launched in rural water supply. A statistical household survey covering 30,000 households has been completed. Housing is not mentioned at all in the review, but in May 1995 a mere 16,000 homes had been built – to be compared with the target of one million by the year 2000.[111]

Some things had been achieved, but only one-third of the budgeted money had been spent by the RDP office. The *Reconstruction and Development Programme* had had a slow start. The budget review presented by the Department of Finance in March the following year was quite explicit on the subject:

> The Presidential Lead Projects have given the Government a range of insights into the development process. They have highlighted the difficulties of working with a bureaucracy unaccustomed to integrated project management, especially in the absence of democratic local government. These systemic shortcomings meant that virtually all RDP projects faced unexpected delays.[112]

In June 1995, the minister responsible for the RDP implementation, Jay Naidoo, formally reported on the program to parliament and then announced plans for a 'National Strategy for Growth and Development' to be finished at the beginning of 1996.[113] Presumably the slow delivery of the RDP was one of the reasons behind the decision to create and *ad hoc* cabinet committee on growth, led by the president himself, in August.[114] It was realized that the RDP would have to be completed with an explicit growth strategy that would ensure that the resources necessary for the successful implementation of the program were forthcoming. The work on the growth and development strategy was begun to carry the RDP forward.[115]

At the same time, it had been discovered that if the RDP was to be successfully implemented, public investment in infrastructure would have to increase almost threefold.[116] A careful quantification had been carried out to see whether the program was feasible given the growth rate prevailing in the economy. The areas covered were energy, water, transport, communications, housing, land reform, health, education, and security. The main scenario (the one more or less corresponding to the RDP targets)

> reflects the preferred expenditure plans of the relevant line departments and public utilities. These were largely derived from two sets of considerations: (1) commercial assessments of projected core infrastructure needs, particularly in the case of the major utilities; and (2) physical assessments in which basic infrastructure backlogs are typically removed within a five year period.[117]

The calculations showed that this scenario required an average growth of infrastructure investment of 21 percent per annum, 'which is above any historical precedent in South Africa'.[118] Furthermore, they indicated that local authorities, i.e. mainly the municipalities, would have to increase their funding of infrastructure with no less than 30 percent each year on average.[119] These requirements were compared with a 'macro-envelope' calculation building on the budget projections of the Department of Finance: a deficit reduction with 0.5 percentage points per annum, constant government spending in real terms and real GDP growth of 3 percent on average. These assumptions allowed for public investment growth of 7.5 percent per annum – far less than the requirements posed by the RDP.[120]

It was clear that the RDP, as originally formulated, was not a viable proposition. Above all, a higher growth rate that could sustain the infrastructural investment required was needed, and the National Strategy for Growth and Development that was in the process of being worked out was aiming at a 6 percent annual growth rate of GDP in the year 2000.[121] This strategy was, however, never finished. At the end of March 1996, the RDP office was closed at short notice in connection with the reshuffle of the cabinet that made Trevor Manuel Minister of Finance. From that point, the Department of Finance took the lead in economic policy making, however, with the long-run development questions falling within the domain of the Vice President, Thabo Mbeki.

The elaboration of a growth and development strategy had also been overtaken by an event in February: the release of a document entitled

*Growth for All*, by the South African Foundation, an organization representing the interests of big business.[122] This document called for a comprehensive reform program that would allow the South African economy to reach its growth potential, somewhere above 5 percent per annum with employment growth in the order of 3.5–4 percent per annum, as opposed to the current trend with real GDP growing at a mere 3 percent and open employment increasing to over 40 percent in 2004. According to the South African Foundation, the transformation would require a policy package with slow monetary expansion and a low budget deficit, cutbacks in government spending, less state intervention in the market mechanism, including rapid privatization of state-owned enterprises, and measures designed to enhance the competitiveness of the South African economy in the world market.

The *Growth for All* document sketches five different pillars that are needed to sustain market-friendly growth. The first one deals with the legal framework. It is acknowledged that reforms are underway that aim at guaranteeing a sound legal system. What is lacking, however, is a firm policy to deal with crime. The second one, which is largely in place already, is the policy framework ensuring macroeconomic stability and liberalization of the financial sector. However, exchange controls should be done away with. The third pillar, efficient government, on the other hand, needs to be constructed through drastic reforms. The budget deficit has to be slashed rapidly, by at least 1.5 percentage points every fiscal year, the tax system needs reform – lower corporate taxes, simplification and increased efficiency in collection, public spending must be streamlined – cut and directed towards growth and poverty alleviation – and a social safety net targeting the poor must be provided. The fourth requirement is one of competitive markets, where deregulation that will increase competition is already underway, but where quick privatization is needed and the labor market (seen as one of the most rigid in the world) needs to be made more flexible in terms of wages, bargaining, and employment practices. The outward orientation of the economy, finally, requires a vigorous export drive, whereas measures ensuring trade liberalization and encouraging foreign investment are gradually put in place.

The South African Foundation is careful to point out that 'unemployment is South Africa's biggest economic challenge.'[123] The road to employment goes mainly through growth but growth alone will not create jobs. For this the labor market must be rendered far more flexible. Collective bargaining in its present form is seen as a measure that tends to act as an obstacle to employment creation. In certain, mainly low-skill, segments of the market, wage levels must be made downwardly flexible, to put wage rates in line with productivity. Otherwise, the unemployed will not be hired and the labor market will not clear. Minimum wage legislation must be avoided.

The second core element in the South African Foundation document is the one dealing with how investment is being created. The point of departure here is that growth is crucially dependent on private investment, but private investment, in turn, will not be forthcoming unless the government emits the right kind of signals to prospective investors through its economic policies. If investors do not see the five pillars being constructed the capital stock will not increase. Foreign investors will choose other countries where they perceive that policy conditions are more favorable. As Nicoli Nattrass has pointed out, key among the signals is the tighter fiscal policy, i.e. reduction of the budget deficit, through a reduction of expenditure, while as the same time the tax revenue is reduced.[124]

The provocative South African Foundation document was soon challenged – head on – by a trade union document called *Social Equity and Job Creation,*[125] which rested on six pillars that differed drastically from those supporting the *Growth for All* strategy. Here as well, employment is brought to the forefront, but the union way to jobs for the masses differs completely from the one advocated by business. The first pillar argues that the state can create jobs through such, partly Keynesian, measures as public works, housing programs, demand expansion, training and land reform. No signals to the private sector are necessary to get the process going. Secondly, the poor must receive more via the government budget and this must be financed by increased taxation of corporations and high-income individuals, while the value added tax on necessities consumed by the poor must be lowered. The workers must also be given more influence in decision making. For this, anti-trust legislation is needed, so that monopolies can be broken up and concentration tendencies reversed. Also, worker rights must be promoted and industrial democracy must be introduced. Finally, somewhat unrelated to the other pillars, the union document calls for the promotion of equity and development internationally.

The union view of what constitutes a desirable economic policy differs fundamentally from that of the South African Foundation. The approach is largely Keynesian, interventionist, with emphasis on fiscal expansion to stimulate demand, and through demand, employment. Accordingly, there is no overwhelming need for a rapid reduction of the budget deficit. This could come gradually. The expenditure side of the budget should concentrate on infrastructure and redistribution, as set out in the RDP. The trade union view also differs sharply from that of the South African Foundation when it comes to how the labor market functions. Wage flexibility is not seen as necessary for growth and employment. On the contrary, keeping wages up makes for high demand as well. If workers are trained, labor productivity and production increase, and inflationary pressures originating in the labor market are avoided. Thus, growth is stimulated and, seeing this, private investment will increase as well. The union document sees no conflict between unemployed, who according to the South African Foundation would benefit from lower wages that would give them a chance to get a job, and employed, who prefer wage increases to employment increases. Instead, it is argued, the latter group supports the former through household transfers and by the demand they generate for goods produced in the informal sector.

### Growth, employment and redistribution

The two documents produced by the South African Foundation and the trade unions provoked responses from three other quarters: Business South Africa, the National African Federated Chamber of Commerce and Industry and a number of civic organizations.[126] Far more important, however, was that in June 1996 a team appointed by the Department of Finance to draft a new macroeconomic strategy had finished its work. The new macroeconomic strategy of the government, *Growth, Employment and Redistribution,* was published.[127] In the same way as the *Growth for All* vision, this document views growth as a necessary condition for both employment and redistribution.

A growth rate of 6 percent is necessary to guarantee that by the year 2000 400,000 jobs are created each year. With the present trend – around 3 percent – no more than 100,000 jobs can be created per annum over the next five years, which in turn would mean that unemployment would reach a level of 37 percent by the turn of the century. By the same token, a growth rate of 3 percent would only allow public spending on social and community services to increase by a maximum of 3 percent per annum, i.e. it would more or less keep an even pace with the growth of the population but not allow for any improvement on a per capita basis.

The government strategy is much closer to that of the South African Foundation than to the union view. Keynesian expansionism is out of question:

An expansionary strategy could be considered. However, even under the most favourable circumstances, this would only give a short term boost to growth since it would be choked off by a rising current account deficit, upward pressure on real wages and curtailment of investment plans. Higher fiscal deficits would also lead to higher inflation and higher interest rates, exacerbating the burden of interest payments on the fiscus. More importantly, in the present climate of instability a fiscal expansion would precipitate a balance of payments crisis. Without deep-rooted reforms, there is no possibility of sustainable accelerated growth.[128]

Instead, the *Growth, Employment and Redistribution* strategy opts for supply-side measures that are intended to stimulate private investment by serving as signals of 'correct' or 'appropriate' government behavior, i.e. behavior that will be conducive to macroeconomic balance and create a stable policy environment. Thus, fiscal policy must be tightened and the budget deficit must be brought down to 4 percent by 1997/98 instead of by 1998/99, as was the original intention. Expenditures will be increasingly concentrated on redistribution. Monetary policy will remain tight as well, to contain inflation.

To stimulate investment more directly, the real exchange rate should be kept at a level which makes South African goods competitive abroad. Exchange controls will be relaxed gradually so as to eventually make for a free flow of capital in and out of the country. These measures will be complemented by continued reforms of trade and industrial policy: a lowering of tariffs to put increased competitive pressure on domestic producers, thereby neutralizing the windfall gain the latter obtained as the value of the rand depreciated during the first half of 1996. Tax incentives are foreseen to stimulate investment, and small and medium-sized firms will receive special support.

The program also envisions a 'restructuration' of public assets, i.e. of such public corporations that are not deemed 'strategic' and cooperation of the state with private interests in such areas as transport and telecommunications. The state will also undertake investment in infrastructure to support regional industrial development and provide municipal and rural services in areas where there are large backlogs it is hoped that this will serve to crowd in private investment as well.

One of the central, and as we will soon see, most controversial areas of the new program is the labor market, where 'a structured flexibility within the collective bargaining system'[129] is aimed for. Exactly what this entails is not clear, but it includes 'greater sensitivity in wage determination to varying capital intensity, skills, regional circumstances and firm size; reduced minimum wage schedules for young trainees, reducing indirect wage costs; and increasing the incentives for more shifts, job sharing and greater employment flexibility'.[130] To make the unions go along, the document finally outlines 'a social agreement to facilitate wage and price moderation, underpin accelerated investment and employment and enhance public service delivery'.[131] The idea is that concessions in the labor market are to be traded for a commitment to keep prices down and to increase investment on part of the employers and one to deliver on the basic needs count on part of the government.

**The rocky road ahead**

Will the new strategy work? This is far from certain. We will next proceed to examine a few crucial features of the *Growth, Employment and Redistribution* document to find out what may possibly go wrong. Let us begin on the growth side, with some variables that are basically outside government control but which are completely central for the outcome: private investment, capital inflows, and non-mineral exports.

The basic assumption with respect to investment is that private investors act from their perception of whether the government does the 'right' or the 'wrong' thing when deciding South Africa's economic policy. If investors are convinced that government policy will succeed in stabilizing the economy they will look to the future with confidence and increase their investment. A reduction of the budget deficit and a continued tight monetary policy in this view demonstrate a determination to get the central macroeconomic variables under control.

But how realistic is such a view? Does investor confidence not have anything to do with incomes and demand? That is hardly the case. Admittedly, if the government policy package is perceived as 'right' it should *ceteris paribus* have an impact on investment, but it may be (1) that this impact is small or (2) that the package has an influence on demand that violates the *ceteris paribus* condition in a way that produces a net negative impact on investment. The most serious of these two objections is the second one, but unfortunately it is not unrealistic. A tightening of the fiscal stance combined with a conservative monetary policy reduces both income and demand and hence the size of the domestic markets for different types of goods and services, and in that situation the question arises as to whether this effect will be stronger or weaker than the signal effect coming from the policy package. If demand is viewed as too feeble it hardly seems likely that investors will respond to 'positive' policy signals. They may simply choose to wait and see whether policies produce growing markets as well.

Related to the investment issue is the issue of foreign capital. For the strategy to work, a capital inflow from abroad on the order of 4 percent of GDP is needed by the year 2000, which entails a gradual increase from an estimated 155 million US dollars in 1996/97 to 804 million in 2000/01. Again, whether this will take place depends entirely on what determines (foreign) investor confidence. Is it really enough to signal that the government will go for macroeconomic stability, or will nothing happen until growth is a proven fact, and where will growth come from in that case?

The third crucial component of the growth part of the strategy is exports. Mineral exports can no longer drive the South African economy and gold mining, in particular, has for several years been experiencing a cost squeeze which has at times been combined with falling world market prices. This problem is recognized both in the RDP and in the new government strategy, where one of the central features is that non-gold (i.e. mainly industrial) exports increase by over 8 percent per annum, rising to over 10 percent at the turn of the century.

Whether this forecast will come true depends mainly on variables over which South Africa has no control, notably how world markets develop. The new strategy contains a trade and industry component, but this can have marginal influence at best. After signing the Marrakesh Agreement and becoming a member of the WTO South Africa can no longer resort to direct export-targeted producer subsidies, as in the GEIS scheme. Thus, only general macroeconomic policy measures and supply-side oriented interventions remain in the tool box of the policy makers.

The macroeconomic policy is more or less in place already. The fall of the value of the rand during the first half of 1996 served to reestablish equilibrium in the foreign exchange market after a period of overvaluation of the currency, and the government intends to avoid overvaluation and the loss of competitiveness that goes with it in the future. The anti-inflationary monetary policy serves to ensure that no real appreciation takes place via a domestic price level that rises faster than those of South Africa's main trading partners. The country has also undertaken to scrap all quantitative import restrictions and unify and reduce its tariff levels until these meet

WTO standards. This process has even been faster than that required by the WTO.

The more interesting part is then to see what may be achieved via the supply-side measures. These measures have been developed gradually during the last five or six years.[132] Today they include marketing support and some schemes that aim specifically at medium-sized and small firms, such as credit facilities either for export orders or in general, and help with employment of consultants in the fields of technology and marketing. Accelerated depreciation schemes and tax holidays are in the process of being introduced.

There is no need to go into any details with respect to these schemes here. It is frequently alleged that small firms are being discriminated against and that no effective support schemes are available for them.[133] Even more important may be that the incentive schemes in operation tend to cover too wide a territory. The list of schemes is long and it pulls in many directions. If too many and too different criteria are employed simultaneously the result may be that funds are spread across too many branches and firms to be effective. Thus, location, labor intensity, and 'priority' considerations will all be employed to determine who qualifies for tax holidays.

If supply-side measures are to have any effect they must concentrate and target a limited number of industries and firms. Essentially, it is a question of 'picking the winners' in the sense that South Africa's comparative advantage in manufacturing must be found (or possibly created). But in which sectors should the investigation start? A recent contribution by Hildegunn Kyvik Nordås points to medium-wage, low-technology, and resource-intensive industries, like non-ferrous metals, iron and steel, paper and printing, and shipbuilding.[134] Non-ferrous metals was the only product category found to be competitive compared to the United States (the country taken to represent the productivity frontier). The other three categories are not directly competitive but have a large potential for exploiting economies of scale in a larger market. Not surprisingly these industries also belong to the least protected categories. Increased liberalization of foreign trade can therefore be expected to reinforce their relative position.

The identified industries are also relatively capital-intensive, which in turn means that further expansion of output is likely to be investment-driven, but this will present a problem:

unless capital investment is accompanied with accumulation of human capital and changes in work organisation, it runs into diminishing returns.

A sustained recovery of investment, and consequently a recovery in manufacturing output growth, cannot be expected unless this precondition is accomplished.[135]

Accumulation of human capital will take considerable time in South Africa. The apartheid system did profound and systematic damage in this respect, and it also affected the possibilities for learning by doing negatively, by posing obstacles to changes in the prevailing work organization on the factory and firm level. Today, a 'shortage of skills and inefficient work organization are problems at all levels of the organization' and 'the industrial environment does not encourage initiatives and learning by doing on the shop-floor.'[136] Thus, in the short and medium run, the exploitation of economies of scale in the resource-intensive industries in the context of a larger market is what offers the most promising road to increased productivity and growth. However, in the longer run, this strategy may turn out to be a dead-end unless it is combined with a systematic accumulation of human capital. Nordås' conclusions are worth quoting at some length:

Scale economies can be improved either through investment in new capacity or by concentrating production on fewer varieties along the horizontal dimension. Unfortunately, exploiting economies of scale on firm or plant level has only a temporary effect on productivity as moving to efficient scale improves the productivity *level*, but has only a short-term effect on the productivity *growth rate*. However, the scale-intensive industries in South Africa are far from the point where economies of scale are exhausted, and potential gains from this source of productivity growth are substantial. Moreover, when concentrating on fewer varieties along the horizontal dimension is combined with intraindustry trade, dynamic economies of scale may arise from a greater variety of inputs, international technological spillovers and increased competition, which in turn could initiate a faster adoption rate of new varieties along the vertical dimension. The latter effect probably depends on south African companies becoming a part of international networks.

The ... most important, albeit time-consuming, source of future productivity growth is investment in human capital. This is a precondition for climbing up the learning curve. The expanding industries are relatively mature, however, and the learning curves relatively flat, but high value added products are found in all industries. If South Africa is able to improve human capital accumulation, and redirect its R&D efforts towards adopting foreign technologies in its competitive or potentially competitive industries, is would probably be able to imitate and further develop new technologies at an earlier stage in the product cycle.[137]

To the extent that Nordås' findings are correct, we may also conclude that the present export-promoting measures will have no or little impact on South African exports. They do not target the right kind of industries and they do not provide support for the right thing. The funds would have made a much better contribution of they had been spent on education and related measures that contribute to human capital accumulation.

The new growth strategy may also be choked by tight stabilization policies. As was pointed out above, in the discussion of monetary policy, combating inflation has been a very high priority during the last few years. This has, however, had its costs, especially in the form of high nominal and real interest rates that act as a hurdle for companies that want to finance an expansion of activities in the capital market. At the end of April 1996 the bank rate was increased to 16 percent.[138] This means that companies would have to pay, say, 25 percent in nominal terms when borrowing, which clearly acts as a deterrent to loan-financed investment. If this situation continues in the future, stabilization may be bought at the expense of growth.

The fall of the external value of the rand made the government opt for speeding up the pace of tariff reductions. This was partly for monetary reasons, as a measure to put pressure on domestic producers to keep prices down, and the *Growth, Employment and Redistribution* document also points to tariff reductions as a way of containing inflation, but if this does not succeed, the burden will again fall on monetary policy. This situation could be triggered in different ways, for example via the skilled labor market or via the balance of payments.

South Africa has suffered from a lack of skilled labor for many years, but skilled labor is one of the factors that will be in high demand if the economy starts to grow at a faster pace than at present. Then an upward pressure will result on skilled wages, but not only that. To the extent that unskilled wage levels are tied to skilled levels through agreements between employers and employees, a 'contamination' effect will result, and a wage-price spiral that calls for monetary and fiscal action will get underway.

The balance of payments situation may also lead to a tightening of monetary policy. Growth in South Africa triggers increased imports and a deficit on the current account. These imports consist not only of capital or intermediate goods that can be used to increase the production of the export industry or the import-competing sectors, and which will hence have a beneficial effect on the payments situation in the somewhat longer run, but also of consumer goods and intermediate products used by producers of non-tradables. Thus, foreign currency will flow out, the rand will tend to depreciate and the rand price of imported inputs will increase and feed domestic inflation. Again, monetary policy is likely to be tightened to defend the rand.

Fiscal policy may also have negative consequences for growth. The new macroeconomic strategy calls for a reduction of the budget deficit and that, as we know, will have to come from the expenditure side. The necessary reductions should ideally take place where they do least harm in terms of efficiency and growth, but in practice, the likely policy is one of across the board cuts, both because of competition between departments and because South Africa does not have the administrative apparatus necessary to identify the least efficient activities during the time span envisaged for the cuts.

**A social accord in the labor market?**

Growth is only the first step in the new strategy. Employment must also be generated in such a way that poverty is reduced. To this end, the strategy emphasizes 'structured flexibility' within a framework given by the collective bargaining system. The growth that has taken place during the present upturn has not generated enough jobs, and unless the labor market is rendered more flexible it is felt that the 400,000 jobs per annum by the year 2000 target will be jeopardized. The most important flexibility is the one that has to do with wages. A solidaristic wage policy would get in the way of increased employment. What the strategy envisages is instead that different sectors, firms, and regions need different wage structures if they are to be competitive and employ people.

This is of course not a message which is popular among the trade unions, which tend to interpret it mainly in terms of wage reductions which are impossible to accept unless some kind of compensation is obtained. This idea is also endorsed in the government strategy, and employment is viewed as so central by the government that a presidential commission on the labor market was appointed in 1995. The commission delivered its report in May 1996.[139]

The solution recommended is a tripartite agreement – a social accord – between unions, employers and government. All three parties should bring something that can be traded to the negotiation table: wages in the case of the unions, prices and investment as far as the employers are concerned, and budget expenditure on part of the government. Wage restraint should be offered against increased investment and price restraint, and the public sector should supplement this deal by social expenditure on the one hand and productivity-enhancing investment in infrastructure on the other. The idea is that this should kill three birds with as many stones. Companies will be more competitive, worker welfare will increase, and the government will no longer have to resort to tight policies on either the monetary or the fiscal side to keep inflation at bay but will be able to take on a more active role when it comes to stimulation the economy.

It is, however, highly doubtful whether the willingness to enter a social accord exists among unions and employers. The incentives are not particularly strong. Employers have a problem getting their act as a coherent player together, for the simple reason that decisions with respect to investment and pricing are made by individual companies and not by employer organizations. Hence, it is easy for individual firms to break whatever promises have been made at the negotiation table unless some policing mechanism can be found. A moral hazard problem exists. This fact provides a clear signal to the worker side as well not to enter into a binding commitment with respect to wages and other working conditions, since very little may come out of it. The situation very much resembles the classical Prisoners' Dilemma, where all the players can be better off if they cooperate but where there are strong incentives to proceed individually, on a collision course, instead.

A second problem with the social accord is that it is not at all clear what wage reductions may bring in terms of increased employment. This is a hotly debated issue. The report of the labor market commission makes reference to estimates of long-run employment elasticities in the order of - 0.7, so that a 10 percent reduction of wages should produce a 7 percent increase in employment.[140] However, this reasoning has been questioned by the ILO report which, argues that there is no need for any special measures since, in practice, employment is much higher than what the most commonly cited official statistics would lead us to believe. Wages are not at all as rigid as argued by the conventional wisdom, especially not in the informal labor market.[141]

Finally, there is the question of what changes in wages can achieve when it comes to reducing inequality and poverty and whether such changes need to be supplemented with other measures as well. In our discussion of these two features of the South African economy we concluded that wage differences are one of the most important determinants on income inequality and that almost half of the inequalities caused by wages stem from households with no wage incomes at all. We also found that unemployment is one of the most important determinants of poverty.

Let us begin with inequality. Murray Leibbrandt and his associates have performed a number of simulation experiments to find out how changes in various income components affect the overall inequality, as measured by the Gini coefficient.[142] This exercise revealed, among other things, that a one percent increase in wages would increase the coefficient by 0.07, i.e. inequality would increase.[143] This is natural, as this increase would only benefit those already employed and should not be taken to imply that a wage reduction would necessarily reduce inequality, since, as Leibbrandt and Haroon Bhorat remark, it all depends on whether wage restraint creates employment or not. If it does not, the effects will be unambiguously negative, because the wages of those employed also provide support for those who have no jobs.[144] Employment creation, in turn, will reduce poverty. As of now, 76 percent of the unemployed South Africans who belong to households with no wage earner are poor (78 percent for Africans, and 84 percent for rural households). Of those who belong to households with one wage earner 53 percent are poor (55 among Africans and 73 in rural areas), and if there are two wage earners in the family the corresponding percentages are 57, 66, and 82. (The higher figures in the latter case are probably due to the fact that no effort was made to control for household size.)

This shows that employment does have an impact on poverty, but the effects may not be dramatic and, in addition, some of the most needy groups may not be reached:

South Africans are not perfectly mobile, or equipped with the skills to take up many of the new positions. Thus, the most needy may not obtain the jobs and job creation may not reduce poverty. For example, there is a large literature showing that poor rural households find it hard to move out of rural areas. And it is unlikely that the unemployed from these rural households could easily compete in urban labour markets. Thus, the plight of the rural unemployed is likely to endure whether wage moderation among the unionised, urban workforce generates urban employment or not. This, in turn, suggests an urgent need to target job creation specifically at the poorest of the poor in the rural areas – perhaps through public works programmes supplying rural infrastructure.

However, the data also shows that rural employment is generally unskilled and poorly paid and therefore the impact of rural employment creation on household poverty is unlikely to be dramatic. Indeed, depending on the precise nature of the wage/unemployment trade-off in rural private sector labour markets, a moderate minimum wage policy that raises the quality of the wage support from those with jobs, and a public works programme that leads to new employment, may be the optimal package for the rural unemployed.[145]

If poverty is to be eradicated, employment creation must be complemented with direct welfare measures.

## Conclusions

The political transition in South Africa has been a successful one – against heavy odds. Both national and local elections have been held under relatively fair circumstances. Presently, the South African economy is also in a period of transition, away from the distorted and unjust system created by the apartheid regime, and towards what will hopefully become a system characterized by equal opportunity, efficiency, and prosperity for all.

The march to prosperity is, however, a long one – a march that the South Africans have barely begun. During the 1970s and 1980s, the economy gradually slided into a long recession which came to an end only in mid-1993, when GDP growth figures for the first time in many years began to keep pace with the growth of the population, and self-sustained growth of the type that leads to steadily increasing incomes is not yet in sight. The agricultural sector has periodically been plagued by unfavorable weather and the gold mining sector has been fighting against high costs and often low prices. Manufacturing and services have fared comparatively better, but not well enough to provide a decisive growth impetus. The level of confidence where investment, domestic as well as foreign, picks up enough to boost the economy has not yet been reached. Unemployment looms large, especially among Africans, and South Africa is struggling to find a comparative advantage in manufacturing that would allow the economy to enter a path of export-led growth that does not build on the traditional, and uncertain, minerals.

After several years of indecision, the ANC in 1994 presented an economic program that was taken over in its entirety by the Government of National Unity that came into power after the elections the same year. This *Reconstruction and Development Programme* is fundamentally a basic needs program that aims at improving the lot of the poor and redressing the inequalities between the races. Unfortunately, the program ran into trouble almost immediately. The administrative structure required to carry it out was not in place and, what is worse, the programs required public investment of a magnitude that is not compatible with the rate of growth prevailing in the economy.

As a result, the government has been forced to revise its economic strategy. In June 1996 a team appointed by the Department of Finance presented a macroeconomic strategy for *Growth, Employment and Redistribution* which attempts to increase the rate of growth of GDP to 6 percent around the year 2000, so as to increase employment and ensure that the targets of RDP can be reached. Whether this will actually be the case is, however, not clear at all. The new strategy depends critically on factors that are outside government control: private investment, non-gold exports, and capital inflow from abroad. Thus, the future of the South African economy remains uncertain. It is far from clear that the ambitions of the ANC-led government can be realized during the next five years.

## Notes

*I would like to acknowledge the assistance of the following persons who all, gave me their valuable time for interviews: Iraj Abedian, Kedar Asmal, Anthony Black, Estian Calitz, Rashad Cassim, Bernie de Jager, Steven Friedman, Gordon Gleimius, Brian Kahn, Les Kettledas, Murray Leibbrandt, David Lewis, Keith Lockwood, Lieb Loots, John Luiz, Barbara Mbine-Barungi, Themba Mhlongo, Terence Moll, Zunaid Moolla, Jayendra Naidoo, Nicoli Nattrass, Philip Nel, Simon Roberts, Maria Ramos, André Roux, Mario Scerri, Charles Simkins, Ben Smit, Servas van der Berg, Ben van Rensburg, Nick Vink and Harry Zarenda. I would also like to thank all the participants in a seminar held at SIDA in December 1996, where the present work was discussed, for constructive comments.

1   The text was approved by the Constitutional Court on 4 December 1996.
2   Nel (1995), pp. 84–85. The quotations are from Huntington (1991), pp. 114, 151.
3   Friedman (1993), p. 13.
4   Lundahl and Moritz (1996), Chapter 5.
5   Cf. the title of Schrire (1992).
6   Nel (1995), p. 88.
7   Cf. the title of Adam and Moodley (1993).
8   Nel (1995).
9   Department of Finance (1996a), (1996b), (1996c).
10  *Restructuring the South African Labour Market* (1996).
11  South African Foundation (1996), *Social Equity and Job Creation* 1996), Business South Africa (1996), National African Federated Chamber of Commerce and Industry (1996), South African National Civic Organisation et al. (1996).
12  Republic of South Africa (1994a), p. 218.
13  South African Reserve Bank (1995a), p. S–128.
14  South African Reserve Bank (1995e), p. 7.
15  South African Reserve Bank (1996b), p. 3.
16  South African Reserve Bank (1993), p. 5.
17  South African Reserve Bank (1995e), p. 7.
18  South African Reserve Bank (1995a), p. 1.
19  South African Reserve Bank (1995e), p. 7.
20  South African Reserve Bank (1996b), p. 3.
21  South African Reserve Bank (1995e), p. 5.
22  Ibid., p. 11.
23  South African Reserve Bank (1996b), p. 5.
24  South African Reserve Bank (1995e), p. 11.
25  South African Reserve Bank (1995b), p. 5.
26  South African Reserve Bank (1995e), p. 12.
27  South African Reserve Bank (1996b), p. 5.
28  International Monetary Fund (1996), p. 2.
29  South African Reserve Bank (1996b), pp. 12–13.
30  South African Reserve Bank (1995c), p. 7, (1996a), p. 3, (1996b), p. 3.
31  Nattrass (1995), p. 858.
32  South African Reserve Bank (1995e), p. 7, (1996a), pp. 3–4.
33  South African Reserve Bank (1995c), pp. 3–4.
34  Ibid., pp. 7–8.

35    South African Reserve Bank (1996b), p. 4.
36    South African Reserve Bank (1995e), p. 8, (1996b), p. 4.
37    South African Reserve Bank (1995c), p. 4, (1995d), p. 5, (1995e), p. 8.
38    South African Reserve Bank (1996b), p. 4.
39    South African Reserve Bank (1995e), p. 15, (1996b), p. 7.
40    South African Reserve Bank (1995e), p. 15.
41    South African Reserve Bank (1996b), p. 7.
42    Project for Statistics on Living Standards and Development (1994), Central Statistical Service (1995).
43    Standing, Sender and Weeks (1996a), Chapter 4.
44    Bhorat and Leibbrandt (1996).
45    Nattrass and Seekings (1996), p. 7.
46    Standing, Sender and Weeks (1996b), p. 3.
47    Standing, Sender and Weeks (1996a), p. 110.
48    Bhorat and Leibbrandt (1996). The poverty line is defined in such a way as to cover the lowest 40 percent of the households, in terms of expenditure per adult equivalent.
49    Nattrass (1996a) provides some criticisms of the ILO argument.
50    Bhorat and Leibbrandt (1996). 'Urban' areas exclude the three 'metropolitan' cities.
51    The remittances category includes 'remittances from absent family members and marital maintenance', wage income derives from 'regular and casual employment and value of benefits such as subsidised housing, transport and food', income from agriculture is defined as 'profit from commercial farming as well as small-scale/subsistence farming for both sale and own consumption', capital income consists of 'dividends, interest, rent income, imputed rent from residing in own dwelling and private and civil (contributory) pensions', state transfers comprise 'social pensions, disability grants, poor relief, unemployment insurance and child maintenance grants' and self employment in the present context means 'informal and formal business activities' (Bhorat, Leibbrandt, and Woolard (1995), p. 3).
52    Ibid., p. 7.
53    Bhorat and Leibbrandt (1996).
54    Ibid.
55    Lundahl and Moritz (1996), p. 96.
56    South African Reserve Bank (1995e), pp. 17–19.
57    South African Reserve Bank (1996b), pp. 8–10.
58    South African Reserve Bank (1995e), p. 16.

59    South African Reserve Bank (1996b), p. 7.
60    South African Reserve Bank (1995e), p. 17, (1996b), p. 8.
61    South African Reserve Bank (1995e), p. 33.
62    South African Reserve Bank (1995e), pp. 33–37, (1996b), pp. 15–17, International Monetary Fund (1996), pp. 21–24.
63    McCarthy (1996), p. 1.
64    Belli, Finger and Ballivian (1993), pp. 20–22.
65    Hirsch (1996), interview with Rashad Cassim, University of Cape Town, 19 July 1996. The quotation is from Hirsch.
66    McCarthy (1996), p. 13.
67    South African Reserve Bank (1995e), p. 22.
68    Lundahl and Petersson (1991), p. 323.
69    McCarthy (1996), p. 17.
70    Ibid., pp. 18–19.
71    Maasdorp (1996), p. 7.
72    South African Reserve Bank (1995e), p. 21.
73    Ibid.
74    Ibid., p. 22.
75    South African Reserve Bank (1996b), p. 12.
76    *Sunday Star* (1996), Klein (1996), Myburgh (1996).
77    South African Reserve Bank (1995e), p. 23.
78    Ibid., p. 24.
79    Ibid., pp. 24–25.
80    Lundahl and Moritz (1996), pp. 77–78.
81    South African Reserve Bank (1995e), pp. 25-26, (1996b), pp. 10–11.
82    South African Reserve Bank (1995e), p. 26, (1996b), p. 12.
83    South African Reserve Bank (1996b), p. S–80.
84    Ibid., p. S–78.
85    South African Reserve Bank (1995e), p. 27, (1996b), p. 13.
86    South African Reserve Bank (1995e), pp. 27–28.
87    South African Reserve Bank (1995e), p. 29, (1996b), p. 13.
88    South African Reserve Bank (1995e), p. 47.
89    Republic of South Africa (1996), p. B.58
90    Ibid., pp. 2–4.
91    South African Reserve Bank (1995e), p. 47.
92    Republic of South Africa (1996), p. B.58.
93    South African Reserve Bank (1995e), p. 47.
94    South African Reserve Bank (1995e), pp. 49–51, (1996b), pp. 22–23.
95    South African Reserve Bank (1995e), pp. 52–53.

96    Republic of South Africa (1996), p. 6–1.
97    ANC (1994).
98    Ibid., p. 6.
99    A capsule history of the steps in this process is given in Lundahl and Moritz (1996), Chapter 14.
100   ANC (1994), p. 20.
101   Ibid., p. 22.
102   Ibid., p. 34.
103   Ibid., p. 41.
104   Ibid., p. 43.
105   Ibid., p. 60.
106   Republic of South Africa (1994b).
107   Lundahl and Moritz (1994), provide a detailed discussion of the scope for redistribution.
108   *Business Day* (1995).
109   Ministry in the Office of the President (1995a).
110   Ibid., p. 2.
111   Palmberg and Strand (1995), p. 154.
112   Republic of South Africa (1996), pp. 2–7.
113   Naidoo (1995).
114   Palmberg and Strand (1995), pp. 215–16.
115   See Inter-Governmental Forum (1995), and Ministry in the Office of the President (1995b), for details.
116   Ministry in the Office of the President (1996).
117   Ibid., p. iii.
118   Ibid., p. iv.
119   Ibid., p. vi.
120   Ibid., p. vii.
121   Ministry in the Office of the President (1995b), p. 4.
122   South African Foundation (1996).
123   Ibid., p. 1.
124   Nattrass (1996b), p. 5.
125   *Social Equity and Job Creation* (1996).
126   Business South Africa (1996), National African Federated Chamber of Commerce and Industry (1996), South African National Civic Organisation et al. (1996).
127   Department of Finance (1996a), (1996b), (1996c).
128   Department of Finance (1996a), p. 3.
129   Ibid., p. 4.

130 Ibid.
131 Ibid., p. 5.
132 *Support Measures for the Enhancement of International Competitiveness of South Africa's Industrial Sector* (1995).
133 Interviews with Keith Lockwood, South African Chamber of Business, Johannesburg, 12 July 1996 and Anthony Black, University of Cape Town, 17 July 1996.
134 Nordås (1996).
135 Ibid., p. 729.
136 Ibid. p. 718.
137 Ibid., pp. 729–30.
138 South African Reserve Bank (1996b), p. 29.
139 *Restructuring the South African Labour Market* (1996).
140 Ibid., pp. 51–52.
141 Standing, Sender and Weeks (1996).
142 Bhorat, Leibbrandt and Woolard (1995), Leibbrandt, Woolard and Woolard (1996).
143 Leibbrandt, Woolard and Woolard (1996), p. 7.
144 Bhorat and Leibbrandt (1996).
145 Ibid.

## References

Adam, Heribert and Moodley, Kogila (1993), *The Negotiated Revolution: Society and Politics in Post-Apartheid South Africa*. Jonathan Ball Publishers: Johannesburg.

ANC (African National Congress) (1994), *The Reconstruction and Development Programme*. Umanyano Publications: Johannesburg.

Belli, Pedro; Finger, Michael and Ballivian, Amparo (1993), *South Africa Review of Trade Policy Issues*. Southern Africa Department, World Bank: Washington, D.C.

Bhorat, Haroon and Leibbrandt, Murray (1996), 'Understanding Unemployment: The Relationship between the Employed and the Jobless', in Baskin, Jeremy (ed.), *Against the Current: Labour and Economic Policy in South Africa*. Ravan Press: Johannesburg.

Bhorat, Haroon; Leibbrandt, Murray and Woolard, Ingrid (1995), 'Towards an Understanding of South Africa's Inequality', Paper Delivered at the African Economic Research Consortium's Conference: Transitional and

Long-term Development Issues, Johannesburg, November 30 to December 1.

*Business Day* (1995), 'Structural Flows Delay RDP Plans', 9 June.

Business South Africa (1996), *Background Document for the 'Social Accord' Process.* Johannesburg.

Central Statistical Service (1995), *October Household Service 1994.* Pretoria.

Department of Finance (1996a), *Growth, Employment and Redistribution: A Macro-Economic Strategy.* Pretoria.

Department of Finance (1996b), *Growth, Employment and Redistribution: A Macro-Economic Strategy (Appendices).* Pretoria.

Department of Finance (1996c), *Growth, Employment and Redistribution: A Macro-Economic Strategy. Summary.* Pretoria.

Friedman, Steven (ed.) (1983), *The Long Journey: South Africa's Quest for a Negotiated Settlement.* Ravan Press: Johannesburg.

Hirsch, Alan (1996), 'Foreword', *Global Trade*, Vol. 3.

Huntington, Samuel (1991), *The Third Wave: Democratization in the Late Twentieth Century.* University of Oklahoma Press: Norman.

Inter-Governmental Forum (1995), *Toward a National Strategic Vision.* 27 November. No place given.

International Monetary Fund (1996), *South Africa - Selected Economic Issues.* SM/96/109, May 10, Washington, D.C.

Klein, Marcia (1996), 'Rand Slides to Two-Month Law', *Sunday Times*, 14 July.

Leibbrandt, Murray V.; Woolard, Christopher D. and Woolard, Ingrid D. (1996), 'The Contribution of Income Components to Income Inequality in South Africa: A Decomposable Gini Analysis', Living Standards Measurement Study, Working Paper No. 125, World Bank: Washington, D.C.

Lundahl, Mats and Moritz, Lena (1994), 'The Quest for Equity in South Africa – Redistribution and Growth', in Odén, Bertil et al., *The South African Tripod: Studies on Economics, Politics and Conflict.* Scandinavian Institute of African Studies: Uppsala.

Lundahl, Mats and Moritz, Lena (1996), *Det nya Sydafrika: Ekonomi och politik efter apartheid.* SNS Förlag: Stockholm.

Lundahl, Mats and Petersson, Lennart (1991), *The Dependent Economy: Lesotho and the Southern African Customs Union.* Westview Press: Boulder, CO.

Maasdorp, Gavin (1996), 'Trade Integration and Economic Development: Some Southern African Issues', Paper prepared at the sixteenth Arne Ryde Symposium, on Post-Apartheid Southern Africa – Economic Challenge and Policies for the Future, Lund, 24–25 August.

McCarthy, Colin (1996), 'South African Trade and Industrial Policy in a Regional Context', Paper prepared for the sixteenth Arne Ryde Symposium, on Post-Apartheid Southern Africa – Economic Challenges and Policies for the Future, Lund, 24–25 August.

Ministry in the Office of the President (1995a), *The RDP: April 27 1995. The First Year Reviewed.* Pretoria.

Ministry in the Office of the President (1995b), *Towards a National Growth and Development Strategy.* Summary of Cabinet Memorandum Nr. 14 of 1995, dated 30th November 1995. Pretoria.

Ministry in the Office of the President (1996), *Towards a National Infrastructural Investment Framework.* Second Draft. 25 March. Pretoria.

Myburgh, Nancy (1996), 'Reserve Bank in Bid to Shore up the Rand', *Business Report*, 15 July.

Naidoo, Jay (1995), *Taking the RDP forward.* Ministry in the Office of the President: Pretoria.

National African Federated Chamber of Commerce and Industry (NAFCOC) (1996), *Growth and Development with Equity Strategy.* Marshalltown.

Nattrass, Nicoli (1995), 'The Crisis in South African Gold Mining', *World Development*, Vol. 23.

Nattrass, Nicoli (1996a), 'Data Must Not Disguise the Need for More Jobs', *Business Day,* 24 June.

Nattrass, Nicoli (1996b), 'Gambling on Investment, Growth and Equity: Competing Economic Visions in South Africa', Department of Economics, University of Cape Town.

Nattrass, Nicoli and Seekings, Jeremy (1996), 'Changing Patterns of Inequality in the South African Labour Market', Paper prepared for the 16th Arne Ryde Symposium, on Post-Apartheid Southern Africa – Economic Challenges and Policies for the Future. Lund, 24–25 August.

Nel, Philip (1995), 'Transition through Erosion: Comparing South Africa's Democratisation', *Aussenpolitik*, Vol. 46.

Nordås, Hildegunn Kyvik (1996), 'South African Manufacturing Industries – Catching Up or Falling Behind?', *Journal of Development Studies*, Vol. 32.

Palmberg, Mai and Strand, Per (1995), *Sydafrika: En regnbågsnation föds.* Scandinavian Institute of African Studies: Uppsala.

Project for Statistics on Living Standards and Development (1994), *South Africans Rich and Poor: Baseline Household Statistics.* South African Labour and Development Research Unit: Cape Town.

Republic of South Africa, Central Statistical Service (1994a), *South African Statistics.* Pretoria.

Republic of South Africa (1994b), *Government Gazette,* Vol. 353, No. 16085, 23 September. Cape Town.

Republic of South Africa, Department of Finance (1996), *Budget Review,* 13 March 1996. No place.

*Restructuring the South African Labour Market* (1996). Report of the Commission to Investigate the Development of a Comprehensive Labour Market Policy. CTP Book Printers: Cape Town.

*Saturday Star* (1996), 'Rand in Spectacular Dive', 13 July.

Schrire, Robert (1992), *Adapt or Die: The End of White Politics in South Africa.* Hurst & Company: London.

*Social Equity and Job Creation: The Key to a Stable Future. Proposals by the South African Labour Movement* (1996). Issued by the labour caucus at Nedlac incorporating Cosatu, Nactu and Fedsal. No place given.

South African Foundation (1996), *Growth for All: An Economic Strategy for South Africa.* Johannesburg.

South African National Civic Organisation (SANCO), South African Federal Council for the Disabled (SAFCD), Women's National Coalition (WNC) and National Rural Development Forum (NRDF) (1996), *Return to the RDP.* No place given.

South African Reserve Bank (1993), *Annual Economic Report 1993.* Pretoria.

South African Reserve Bank (1994), *Quarterly Bulletin,* No. 194, December.

South African Reserve Bank (1995a), *Quarterly Bulletin,* No. 195, March.

South African Reserve Bank (1995c), *Quarterly Bulletin,* No. 197, September.

South African Reserve Bank (1995d), *Quarterly Bulletin,* No. 198, December.

South African Reserve Bank (1995e), *Annual Economic Report 1995.* Pretoria.

South African Reserve Bank (1996a), *Quarterly Bulletin,* No. 199, March.

South African Reserve Bank (1996b), *Quarterly Bulletin,* No. 200, June.

Standing, Guy; Sender, John and Weeks, John (1996a), *Restructuring the Labour Market: The South African Challenge*. Preliminary version. International Labour Office: Geneva.

Standing, Guy; Sender, John and Weeks, John (1996b), *Restructuring the Labour Market: The South African Challenge – Executive Summary*. Preliminary version. International Labour Office: Geneva.

*Support Measures for the Enhancement of the International Competitiveness of South Africa's Industrial Sector* (1995), Submission by Government to the Trade and Industry Chamber of Nedlac, 16 November. No place given.

# 6 The new South Africa: growth or stagnation?*

South Africa's second post-apartheid elections are scheduled for 1999. By then, the African National Congress (ANC) will have been in power for five years, nominally at the head of a Government of National Unity, together with the National Party (until April 1996) and Inkatha, but in fact carrying out a purely ANC policy agenda. Coming to power on the crest of rising expectations among the black majority, the ANC failed only by a narrow margin to obtain the two-thirds majority that would have made it possible for it to rule alone.

The apartheid era, from the triumph of the National Party in the 1948 elections to the release of Nelson Mandela and other political prisoners in early 1990 saw the creation of the most elaborate system of economic and social discrimination in world history. Discrimination was not new in South Africa, however, having been a feature of that part of the African continent since the arrival of the first European settlers in 1652. What was new in 1948 was the systematic thoroughness with which discriminatory legislation was pursued. The results were evident at each and every level of society, permeating all facets of everyday life. In the end, the economic costs of the system were huge: low efficiency, low growth, isolation from the international economy, and low incomes, malnutrition, ill health, bad housing and inferior education for the black majority.

Thus for more than forty years the rights and economic opportunities of the majority of the South African population were constrained by the National Party government. All available indicators tell an identical story: there was an enormous gap between whites and blacks, with Asians and Coloreds somewhere in between. Then, in 1990, the tide began to turn.

National Party president, Frederik Willem de Klerk, finally realized that the apartheid system had no role to play in the new dispensation and had to be relegated to history. The road to democratization lay open and could not be closed again. Once opened, the initiative quickly went into the hands of the ANC. After forty years in power, the National Party was seriously burdened by its tumultuous past. It was incapable of projecting a credible view of what the new South Africa should look like. The task of wooing voters to its side on the basis of well argued political and economic programs proved formidable. There was thus little it could do but fall in line, hoping to salvage something by participating in a government of transition.

This chapter will examine some of the most important economic issues confronting the new leaders in South Africa. The ANC made a number of promises during the 1994 elections, most fundamentally dealing with redistribution, to be implemented up to 1999. They were spelled out in the ANC's economic strategy called the *Reconstruction and Development Programme* (RDP), subsequently adopted by the Government of National Unity. The RDP is essentially a strategy for narrowing the gap between the rich and the poor, with its goals formulated in terms of extending access to education, housing, electricity, water, sanitation, health services and land.[1]

**Background**

In the years that passed between de Klerk's decision to open the democratic process to all South Africans, irrespective of race, and the 1994 elections, the scope for and the economic limitations on redistribution were thoroughly examined by South African economists. The verdict was fairly unanimous: unless drastic measures were resorted to, the scope for a static redistribution of income was small. If the visions contained in the RDP were to be realized, the economy needed to grow and at a much higher rate than before.[2]

The inter-racial distribution problem has been better analyzed than virtually any other economic problem that South Africa faces.[3] I will, therefore, not dwell on it in any detail here. Instead, I will focus on the necessary (but not sufficient) condition for greater equality: growth. How can the ANC-led government inject new life into an economy that was in decline from the 1970s to 1993 and which, thereafter, has only had a rate of growth that barely matched that of the population?[4] An economy that seeks increased income equality via redistribution needs to generate growth. There is simply no way around it.

The year 1999 will be a historical one for South Africa in the sense that it will mark the end of the transition to democratic majority rule. The winner of the parliamentary elections will then form a government without having to pay any political dues to the minority. The winner – the ANC – will take everything. Whatever happens on the road to 1999, the ANC will win a comfortable victory, simply because no alternatives have emerged since 1994 to threaten its dominance. The National Party will be relieved to get half the number of seats it obtained in 1994. With de Klerk gone and its name smeared, the party will gradually fade out of the picture. No serious liberal alternative exists, and no such alternative is likely to emerge in the near future. But even if one should exist by 1999, it would not be able to make much of a dent in the ANC ranks. Inkatha remains an ethnically based party, one which stands and falls with its leader Buthelezi. No populist splinter group has broken away from the ANC. This situation is unlikely to last but requires a trigger in the form of a cataclysmic event. So far, no such occasion has presented itself, and it is unlikely to come before the elections.

The ANC thus rules supreme. It does not have to discuss its policies with other parties unless it wants to. But, as we will demonstrate below, the probability that the present economic strategy will fail to deliver the promised results is very high. Then, possibly, another policy package will have to be tried. However, in the absence of credible political threats to the ANC hegemony, the changes will be marginal, perhaps even cosmetic. Some strategy for the twenty-first century must be put in place before the elections, because the voters will demand it. It will not mean that the preferences of the voters will have changed, however. They will still demand satisfaction of their basic needs, the cornerstone of the Reconstruction and Development Programme. It is hardly realistic to expect any abrupt about turn with regard to how these needs will be met.

Thus growth will be the overriding economic consideration up to the 1999 elections, and quite probably after that as well. In 1999 Nelson Mandela will resign as president and Thabo Mbeki will take over. *Ceteris paribus*, that is not likely to lead to any other changes in economic policy than would have resulted otherwise. Being ultimately responsible for the recent development policy, Mbeki represents continuity, not change.

## Getting growth going

Arguments about to how to get growth going in South Africa have not been lacking. The country has a long and not very successful experience of import substitution in manufacturing, from the 1920s until the change of policy in recent years.[5] In spite of this, when the ANC's economic policy began to take shape after 1990, one of the most favored ideas was that growth could spring out of industrialization based on the domestic market.[6] The demand in this market, if suitably stimulated, would be directed mainly towards low-price necessities that could be produced with the aid of labor-intensive techniques that furthermore would demand few imported inputs. This would create a virtuous spiral, with increasing incomes leading to increasing demand and output. For that to materialize, however, demand would first have to be stimulated. Arguments were thus advanced for a redistribution-driven 'kickstart' of the economy. Construction of dwellings for low-income earners on a large scale being a good example. The sector does not require a huge volume of imported inputs while it is at the same time labor-intensive.

Although the kickstart idea was partly based on the existence of un-utilized capacity in labor-intensive sectors, such as construction, it is obvious that when these sectors expand their output, they may have to use intermediates and other inputs from sectors where there is little such capacity, thus inhibiting growth. Also, nothing guarantees that the demand generated by the increased incomes will be directed exclusively towards goods produced in sectors with excess capacity. Thus to what extent it is possible to kickstart the economy is an empirical question.

In 1989, the average capacity utilization in manufacturing was 84.5 percent, not much lower than the 86.3 percent reached in 1981 – a year with high gold prices and insignificant balance of payments restrictions.[7] In 1995 the figure was 83 percent.[8] However, restrictions on the growth rate could also come from imports. At the beginning of the 1990s a one percent increase in domestic expenditure, on average, increased imports by almost 2.2 percent.[9] Thus, in the worst scenario, the kickstart process would be held back by balance of payments difficulties as well.

An alternative way of generating growth that has been suggested is a change in demand patterns, triggered by a redistribution of income and wealth in favor of black South Africans. The latter are believed to spend relatively more on labor-intensive domestically produced goods, and less on imports than whites. The Development Bank of Southern Africa has suggested that incomes spent by Africans tend to yield a contribution to GDP that is almost 21 percent higher than that from incomes spent by whites. Further, black consumption is 21 percent more labor-intensive and 4 percent less import-intensive than that of whites.[10]

Whether a redistribution-driven demand increase generates growth is to a very large extent determined by what happens on the production side. For example, will the output pattern adjust easily when the demand side of the economy emits signals that differ from those of the past? If not, growth will not easily be generated. Unfortunately, there seem to be good reasons for suspecting that adjustment may be sluggish. Here the extent of excess capacity is of fundamental importance, but obstacles may arise in other ways as well. For example, it may not be easy to shift from capital-intensive to labor-intensive methods of production. Elasticities of substitution may be low, at least in the short run, which is the relevant time spectrum if the aim is to kickstart the economy.

The assumptions with respect to demand made by the kickstart and domestic market advocates have also been questioned. Poor people do not necessarily demand mainly labor-intensive goods. Branches of industry like non-electrical appliances, furniture, clothing, leather and metal products, shoes and food are all products would be suitable for small-scale, labor intensive production, but since the income elasticities of demand for most of these do not exceed one, concentrating on them may slow down the kickstart process.[11]

Critics have also pointed out that the idea of growth from redistribution has much in common with the 'macroeconomic populism' of the type practiced in some Latin American countries in the recent past, on the basis of deficit financing via the government budget.[12] The expansion process works only during the initial phase when, in addition, real wages and employment both increase, inflation is kept low through price controls and imports are resorted to in order to ease the bottlenecks created by the increasing demand. In the second phase the country runs out of foreign exchange, and the bottlenecks become visible. The price level increases, the currency appreciates in real terms, and the investment level falls, while real wages remain high. The government budget deficit increases but the rate of growth declines. Finally, the country enters a balance of payments crisis, the currency reserves are almost wiped out, shortages of goods ensue and the budget deficit and the rate of inflation both increase rapidly, while the tax base is simultaneously eroded. Increased foreign support becomes necessary to maintain growth. Since this is often not forthcoming, the economy heads for macroeconomic chaos, and drastic medicine is required to stabilize it. Stagnation sets in.

For whatever reason, the kickstart advocates failed to convince the Government of National Unity that their case was a good one. During the last few years – with a couple of exceptions[13] – the idea of growth from redistribution has faded into the background. This, however, does not mean that the growth theme has been abandoned – on the contrary, it has been given added emphasis – only that now most of the participants in the South African economic debate appear to be convinced that causality runs, or must run, in the opposite direction: from growth to redistribution. According to this view, the task of economic policy is to stimulate growth directly. Only then will South Africa see a rise in employment and incomes as well as increased scope for redistribution in favor of poor population segments.

The 'growth first' strategy has been accepted by the ANC. The *Reconstruction and Development Programme*[14] also has as one of its main objectives the increase of the growth rate to around 5 percent by the turn of the century. Though the RDP is fundamentally a basic needs program, it was realized that without growth the scope for redistribution and poverty reduction would be extremely limited. The program can also be seen as 'a version of a home-grown structural adjustment programme'.[15] The strategy builds on a revision of the trade and industry policy, in the direction of increased openness, increased human capital formation through education and a consistent and growth-fomenting macroeconomic policy. Measures should be devised to stimulate manufacturing exports, increase competitive pressure by lowering tariffs and instituting anti-trust legislation. Small and medium-size enterprises were to be targeted for support: capacity building, training, technological development, infrastructure, marketing, etc. Fiscal and monetary restraint was also seen as contributing to a stable policy environment, conducive to an inflow of foreign capital.

The RDP never got off the ground, however.[16] Lack of capacity at the local level, where the projects were to be implemented, made it fall behind schedule from the very outset. By mid-1995, the office responsible for the implementation of the RDP had discovered that virtually all basic needs projects were behind target. Lacking a clear and coordinated implementation program, the initiative had been left to the individual government ministries, and had thus taken place only in a very *ad hoc* fashion. But the RDP was also overtaken by events. Alternative or complementary strategies were formulated at the same time, reducing the RDP's focus and thrust. Plans were announced, for example, for a national growth and development strategy that would ensure that the resources necessary for the delivery would be forthcoming.

At the same time, the South African Foundation, representing big business, had produced its own growth document, *Growth for All*, where a major economic reform program was sketched.[17] The point of departure was clearly in line with the RDP: the need for an annual growth rate of around 5 percent if employment was to increase by 3.5–4 percent, so as to avoid an open unemployment rate of 40 percent or more in 2004. The *Growth for All* strategy rested on five pillars: (1) law and order, (2) macroeconomic stability and financial liberalization (notably the scrapping of exchange controls), (3) a reduction of the budget deficit by at least 1.5 percentage points per year, tax cuts and reforms, (4) increasingly competitive markets, with deregulation and privatization, as well as increased wage flexibility in the labor market and, finally, (5) measures to liberalize foreign trade and encourage an inflow of foreign capital. All the pillars were not of equal importance. Two elements stood out as central: wage flexibility to ensure that employment increased and contraction of the budget deficit through a reduction of government expenditure in order to signal to investors (especially foreign ones) that macroeconomic stability would prevail in the future.

As could be expected, the *Growth for All* strategy did not appeal to the trade union movement, notably the Congress of South African Trade Unions (COSATU). The unions were not late in producing a counter-strategy: *Social Equity and Job Creation* (1996). This strategy proceeded very much along Keynesian lines, putting emphasis on the ability of the state to create jobs without having to woo the private sector by stimulating demand and employment via fiscal expansion. Hence the unions argue that there is no need for a rapid tightening of fiscal policy, especially not via the expenditure side. Instead, the taxation of high-income earners and corporations should increase, with proceeds used for transfers and other welfare-increasing measures in favor of the poor. The unions did not see any need for wage flexibility either. On the contrary, high wages would keep demand up, and worker training could be used to increase labor productivity so as to keep cost-push inflationary pressure at bay.

Two opposing growth strategy proposals had thus been produced. In the meantime it had also become clear that with the prevailing growth rate the RDP stood little chance of being implemented according to the envisaged timetable. For that, investment in infrastructure would have to grow with 21 percent per annum and the local authorities (municipalities etc.) would have to increase their infrastructure funding with no less than 30 percent each year. With a growth rate of GDP of 3 percent, constant government spending and a reduction of the budget deficit of 0.5 percentage points per year, that level of expenditure was completely out of question. If the RDP was to be saved the growth rate had to be increased. The question was: how?

The ANC-led government by and large opted for the solution suggested by the South African Foundation. In June 1996 a new macroeconomic strategy was ready: *Growth, Employment and Redistribution* (GEAR).[18] The growth target is roughly the same: around 6 percent per annum at the turn of the century. Central in the new strategy is the signaling aspect: by demonstrating that a consistent, stabilizing macroeconomic policy is firmly implemented, investor confidence in South Africa is bound to increase. The slashing of the budget deficit is to be accelerated and monetary policy is to remain tight. Investment will be stimulated by tax incentives, and a gradual relaxation of exchange rate controls to enable free movement of capital. To ensure competitiveness in the world market, tariffs will continue to be lowered. Further, a number of public corporations will be privatized and the state will instead concentrate on the provision of infrastructure. By and large, the idea that greater flexibility, notably with respect to wages, is needed in the labor market has also been accepted, but this flexibility is to be traded for price restraint and job-creating investment on part of employers.

**Growth: the actual record**

The 1970s and 1980s were bad years for the South African economy. Between 1970 and 1985 the real growth rate of GDP was a mere 2.6 percent per annum on average – barely enough to match the rate of population growth.[19] By the mid-1980s growth rates were negative. The figures for the latter half of the 1980s were positive, but below 2 percent on average,[20] while in 1990–92 economic decline set in, continuing until 1993.[21] The ensuing recovery has, however, proved to be highly uneven. Thus while the growth rate jumped to an (annualized) 6 percent during the latter half of 1993,[22] it was only 1.5 percent on an annual basis for the year. In 1994 it grew by 2.5 percent, rising to 3.5 percent in 1995, but then fell to 3 percent in 1996.[23]

This relative improvement also conceals substantial fluctuations, with a decline of 1 percent during the first half of 1994, followed by a 5.5 percent expansion over the rest of the year.[24] There was then a somewhat steadier expansion of 3.5 percent, 2.5 percent, 3.5 percent, 3 percent and 3.5 percent over the ensuing six-month periods to the end of 1996, and another dip to a mere 1 percent during the first half of 1997.[25] With a population growth rate of around 2.2 percent per annum[26] these growth rates are not impressive. In *per capita* terms, the one for 1994 is virtually naught and the next two years yielded a mere 0.8–1.3 percent *per capita* growth. Using the higher figure, it would take over fifty years to double *per capita* income in South Africa, while with the lower figure it would take over eighty years. Should the slowdown that began in 1997 continue, the time horizon will have to be stretched even more.

The recovery initiated in 1993 began on a broad basis, with strong growth in the secondary and tertiary sectors. Agricultural output has gone through a number of swings caused by variable weather conditions. In 1993 production increased by no less than 29 percent, followed by a 12 percent increase in 1994.[27] Severe drought, leading to food imports in 1994, led to a 15 percent fall in agricultural output, followed in 1996 by a 26 percent increase, due to exceptionally good weather. In the first half of 1997 an annualized decline of 21 percent was projected.[28] Thus, what happens in agriculture is ultimately conditioned by the weather.

Gold mining has been a consistently weak performer, with a negative contribution to overall growth throughout 1994–96. In the latter year gold output reached its lowest level in forty years. The gold content of the ore is falling and mining itself is done at deeper and deeper ground levels, increasing the risks and costs of the operation.[29] This is hardly a sector that will be a strong propagator of growth in the future. Generally speaking, non-gold mining has fared better, but mining output as a whole is sensitive to international price movements, as witnessed during the second half of 1996.[30]

Outside the primary sector, output performance has been better from the second quarter of 1993 to the second quarter of 1995, with manufacturing displaying the highest growth rate. Thereafter, output slackened, as household demand weakened and inventory accumulation was reduced. The year 1996 was an almost stagnant one. The depreciation of the rand during most of 1996, however, prepared the ground for a renewed expansion in 1997.[31] Construction, in turn, has contributed only modestly, with growth rates of 1.5–2 percent, among other things because of a late start during the upturn, but also due to slower than expected expansion of demand from the RDP program. The utilities sub-sector of electricity, gas and water, on the other hand, has expanded rapidly, with growth rates reaching 3.5 percent in

1994/95 to 5 percent thereafter. This has mainly been the result of the extension of the national grid to formerly disadvantaged areas.[32]

The growth rate in the tertiary sectors, finally, has also increased, from about 2.5 percent up to 1995 and 3–3.5 percent, thereafter, before falling during the first half of 1997. Transport and communication and commerce have displayed the highest growth rates, with financial services slightly behind. However, as demand has weakened and production elsewhere in the economy has experienced weaker growth these sectors have also slowed down considerably.[33]

It is readily seen from this cursory overview that the recent growth performance has been both weak and uneven. Recorded growth rates have improved *per capita* incomes only marginally. In a situation where there are strong and repeated demands for substantial redistribution, such growth levels are far from sufficient. Virtually all observers and political actors agree that it is not an acceptable state of affairs. The sectoral composition of growth also gives cause for concern. What happens in agriculture cannot be controlled too much. Gold mining, once the engine in the economy, has shrunk to the point where it now accounts for a mere 2.5 percent of GDP,[34] a share likely to fall further. The output of other minerals is crucially dependent on what happens in the world market. Tertiary sector production is intimately connected with the overall level of economic activity. This leaves manufacturing, and it is around it that the growth debate has centered. Already in 1950 manufacturing had become the largest sector of the economy in terms of output,[35] partly as a result of the import substitution process referred to above.[36] However, long before 1994 this process had run its course. Besides, in April that same year South Africa had signed the Marrakesh Agreement establishing the World Trade Organization. As a result, the import substitution road had for all practical purposes been closed. New ways of expanding the manufacturing sector had to be found. It is in this light that the GEAR strategy is of significance.

GEAR makes clear predictions with respect to growth up to the year 2000.[37] A base scenario[38] assumes a 9.6 percent depreciation of the real exchange rate for 1996 and very small changes after that, and a gradual reduction of the budget deficit up to a level of 3 percent of GDP in fiscal 2000/01. Further, a reduction of government consumption is assumed, along with a reduction of tariffs from 10 percent of import value to 8 percent. Real wage increases in the public sector of 1 percent per annum are coupled with increased public capital formation (with 2–3 percent per year), positive, but falling real interest rates and modest (1.4 percent per annum) private wage increases. These assumptions would generate overall growth rates of 3.3 percent in 1996, 2 percent in 1997, 2.5 percent in 1998, 2.9 percent in 1999 and 3.3 percent in 2000, i.e. rates that would not be able to ensure positive *per capita* income growth for three of the five years in the projection. This is clearly insufficient. At these rates, the *Reconstruction and Development Programme* is in jeopardy.

The GEAR strategy attempts to speed up the growth rate up by introducing the following changes as compared to the base scenario: (1) Faster reduction of the budget deficit, to 4 percent (instead of 4.5) in 1997, 3.5 percent in 1998 and 3 percent in 2000. (2) Accelerated tariff reform, substantial increases in public investment, up to a growth rate of almost 17 percent in 2000 for public authorities (against 2.4 in the base run) and 10 percent in public corporations (against 3 percent). (3) Also included are reduced wage increases in the private sector, confining increases to 0.7 percent per annum, and increased non-gold exports (a growth rate of 10 percent by 2000, against 5.3, in the base scenario). (4) Finally, substantial increases in private investment are assumed (growth rate of 17 percent, against 7.1 in the base scenario) as well as increased foreign capital inflows, in the form of direct investment, rising from 155 million US dollars in 1996 to 804 million in 2000. Supposedly, this medicine would increase GDP growth to 3.5 percent in 1996, 2.9 percent in 1997, 3.8 percent in 1998, 4.9 percent in 1999 and 6.1 percent in 2000.[39]

But will it? As we have seen, the actual growth rate for 1996 was 3 percent, not 3.5 percent, and the annualized rate for the first half of 1997 falls far short of the GEAR target for the year as a whole. Will the same pattern prevail in the future – that is, with actual growth rates falling persistently below those predicted in the accelerated GEAR scenario? Unfortunately there are good reasons to fear that such may be the case.

## Why GEAR won't work I: the investment problem

The main snag regarding GEAR is that it builds on a number of variables which, from the point of view of the government, are by and large exogenous. The most important is investment. The government attempts to get growth going through an expansion of private investment, but, to the extent that private investors want to witness growth before they invest, we are back to square one. This is obviously a chicken-and-egg problem, certainly a vicious circle, and there is no obvious way of breaking it. The problem manifests itself in several ways. We shall deal with each one in turn, beginning with the determinants of investment.

What determines investment is a tricky question in any economy, while the South African case presents more complications than most. Basically, investment is a matter of expectations with respect to the future. If investors are not confident that the future will be favorable, they will not invest. The question is then how confidence is built. What do investors look at when they form their expectations? The GEAR strategy makes very definite assumptions about what governs this process: government policy. By emitting the right kind of signals the government can convince both domestic and foreign investors (notably the latter) that a policy environment which is likely to be conducive to stability will prevail. These signals induce investment.

An alternative interpretation runs in terms of 'crowding out'.[40] Increased fiscal discipline will reduce the need for public sector borrowing and this will in turn exert a downward pressure on interest rates that will allow companies in the private sector to finance their expansion. This, however, presupposes that the demand for investment funds is sensitive to changes in interest rates. In a situation where it is highly uncertain what the future will bring, this elasticity may be low and little new investment results. Thus the mechanism that is supposed to trigger investment may be lacking. Furthermore, the GEAR scenario predicts that falling interest rates will go hand in hand with an increased deficit on the current account of the balance of payments, covered by a capital inflow from abroad. Given the recent history of monetary policy in South Africa, this is hardly a likely sequence of events. Still, deterioration of the current account is likely to lead to a tightening of the monetary policy, with higher, not lower, interest rates.

Fiscal austerity and low interest rates are two possible ways of getting investment going. Neither will work in isolation. As noted above, investors may also want to see signs of growth, because growth implies market opportunities.[41] Nobody is likely to invest in an economy heading for a stagnant future. This is a balanced growth *cum* free rider problem. If all investors are waiting for all other investors to get their act together, nothing will happen. To what extent then does government policy have an influence on growth independently of that which goes via government-induced private investment? The GEAR answer is: 'Through exports.' GEAR is a strategy for the open economy, and the government envisages a stimulus to exports that works through three different routes: exchange rate policy, labor market flexibility and tax incentives and other supply-side measures.

The first measure is already in place. From January to November 1996 the rand underwent a depreciation (from an initial overvaluation) *vis-à-vis* the dollar from R3.64 to R4.70.[42] This windfall gain for exporters was complemented with compensating tariff decreases to ensure that resources do not flow into import-competing industries instead of into exports and to maintain competitive pressure in the economy.

The other two measures are much more problematic. In May 1996 a presidential commission on labor market policy presented a report entitled *Restructuring the South African Labour Market*. It is an 'accord' on employment and growth that would bring about the necessary labor market flexibility. The idea is to arrive at a negotiated tripartite solution – a tit-for-tat – between labor, employers and government. Each of the three parties is supposed to bring something to the negotiation table: moderate wage demands (and other demands related to working conditions) in the case of the unions, price restraint and increased investment in that of the employers' organizations and social service and infrastructure provision in the case of the state. This construction does not solve the problem, because it *assumes* that investment will be forthcoming in a situation where exports are, on their own, a crucial element in generating the growth needed for higher investment. We end up in a chicken-and-egg situation again. The reasoning becomes circular.

This is not the only problem with a social accord. It may never come into being, because the negotiators may fail to deliver what it stipulates or simply because they doubt each other's ability to honor it. The fragile link in the accord chain is the employers. Business in South Africa hardly speaks with a single voice. The large corporations to a large extent speak for themselves, while on the more organized collaborative level there are the South African Chamber of Business, the South African Foundation and others. Who then speaks for 'business'? Even if a 'player' with some kind of mandate can be located or constructed there is no guarantee that what is decided at the negotiating table will be honored by the individual companies. In a market economy decisions with respect to investment and pricing are made at the firm level, not centrally. Unless firms believe in the future they will not invest or refrain from raising prices if they cannot cover their costs. This, of course, the labor movement realizes. Business will not be able to come up with a credible commitment. Hence there would be no point in attempting to negotiate a social pact. Once more, the mechanism that is supposed to put investment in motion is missing.

This leaves us with the supply-side measures. Such measures have already been attempted. Between 1990 and mid-1997 a *General Export Incentive Scheme* (GEIS) was in existence. To what extent this scheme, which targeted exports directly and encouraged the use of local inputs, actually managed to stimulate exports is still debatable. Critics claim that its effects were marginal at best – no less than 75 percent of the payments went to the iron and steel industry[43] – and that the support went to the wrong kind of firms, sometimes fraudulently. At any rate, GEIS had to be phased out, since the direct targeting of exports violates the WTO statutes. New measures had to be devised, including accelerated depreciation on new investments, tax holidays, support to small and medium-size firms, marketing support, credit schemes, technological development, etc. Whether these new efforts will be more fruitful than the GEIS scheme remains to be seen. However, since the net appears to have been cast too widely across branches and firms, and with the aid of too many (sometimes possibly conflicting) criteria, this is hardly likely to be the case.[44] Successful targeting requires a good crystal ball. Sectors, subsectors and individual product lines where South Africa has a comparative advantage must be found. This is not an easy exercise, hardly one likely to be conducive to short-run growth. If it works at all, it would do so in the medium to long run.

It is also possible that the wrong industries are being targeted. Recent research indicates that South Africa's comparative advantage is to be found in resource-intensive, low technology and medium-wage industries, like those of non-ferrous metals, iron and steel, paper and printing and shipbuilding. All these are also relatively capital-intensive, which means that expansion of output may be dependent on investment – both in terms of physical capital and in the form of the human capital required to handle the equipment.[45] If so, the conclusions are clear. (1) The best supply-side measure would be education. (2) Once more we are facing the problem of how to get investment going. The present supply-side measures do not seem able to do the trick.

The role of the foreign trade sector appears peculiar once imports are taken into account. GEAR envisages an increase in the deficit on the current account of the balance of payments up to the year 2000.[46] In a simple national income identity setting, the impact of this on the growth rate is *negative*, not positive.[47] How exports work in the GEAR framework is impossible to say, since the underlying model, for some strange reason, has never been made public.

A final question mark has to do with the targeting of foreign investment. At present, foreign capital is flowing into the economy,[48] but it is the 'wrong' kind of capital: either portfolio investment or replacements of the capital stock that was run down during the years of sanction. There is little net expansion of direct investment. It might have made more sense to primarily target domestic firms instead. That South Africa should be able to attract foreign direct investment without growth of domestic capital formation does not sound a likely proposition. Foreign investors are likely to watch the behavior of domestic investors very closely. Thus to the extent that investment picks up one would expect domestic companies to take the lead and foreign companies to follow suit once they are convinced that the economic environment is safe, sound and conducive to future growth.

## Why GEAR won't work II: built-in policy brakes

Investment is not the only problem with the GEAR strategy. It is simply the first hurdle. Assuming that investors react the way GEAR predicts they will, and that growth somehow gets going, a second line of obstacles awaits to be overcome: the austere fiscal policy needed to reduce the budget deficit, and the tight monetary policy that has characterized the South African economy for close to a decade. There is a considerable risk that short-run stabilization considerations will conflict with the growth target.

Already the basic scenario of GEAR calls for a continuous reduction of the government budget deficit, with 0.5 percentage points (of GDP) per annum, to 4.5 percent in 1997 and a final 3.0 percent in 2000. The GEAR strategy for accelerated growth envisages an even faster convergence path, with a reduction in 1997 that is twice as large as in the base run. This would be followed by 0.5 percentage point reductions thereafter, in order to arrive at the 3.0 percent target already by 1999.[49] The higher-growth scenario would thus call for a much more contractionary fiscal stance than the one prevailing in the low-growth one.

Seen in an international perspective, South Africa is not a low-tax economy. The share of taxes in GDP is on the same level as that prevailing, on average, in countries with similar *per capita* income.[50] Whether the tax base can be broadened and existing taxes can always be debated. What matters in the present context is that the central element of GEAR is increased private investment and that the way to higher investment is via the emission of the right signals. This effectively precludes tax increases and puts the entire burden of adjustment on the expenditure side.

Relying on expenditure cuts creates problems. First, they should in principle be made in such a way as to minimize the harmful effects on growth, i.e. the cuts should be selective and target some expenditures and budget votes more than others. In practice, however, such targeting tends to be difficult. Government departments tend to watch each other and defend their own territories. In this situation the likelihood that the cuts will be effected in an 'egalitarian' way, that is without regard for efficiency and growth considerations, is high.

Should the economy grow more slowly than expected, the problem will be compounded. The computations for government revenue build on some assumed growth path of GDP. Thus if the actual rate falls short of that targeted, revenues will fall short of target as well. This implies, in turn, that, if the targeted budget reduction is to materialize, expenditures must be reduced at a faster rate than planned. Thus the policy becomes more contractionary than originally intended, public investment suffers and the burden of 'getting growth going' through investment will increasingly be placed on the shoulders of the private sector. The use of tax holidays to stimulate growth has similar effects. They reduce potential revenue and shift the burden of adjustment to the expenditure side. On the other hand, situations could arise where companies create new firms or subsidiaries just to be able to continue to enjoy tax holidays.

Unless education is exempted, the expenditure cuts will also hamper human capital formation, in a situation where skilled labor is badly needed. The apartheid legacy has implied an acute shortage of skilled people. From the mid-1970s onwards, this has contributed to the poor growth.[51] This shortage, which, as we have seen, may have serious consequences for export growth, still persists and to the extent that expenditure cuts take place across the board will be exacerbated.

The skill issue takes us from fiscal to monetary policy. For a number of years, monetary management has been tight. In 1989 the South African Reserve Bank tightened the monetary screw in a bid to defend the rand. This tight policy still prevails. The autonomy of the bank is guaranteed in the new constitution, which means that since the main task of monetary policy is that of combating inflation the bank could easily pull in a direction that is likely to hamper growth. Contractive action can be set off in different ways, and one of them is via the skill constraint. Growth increases the demand for skilled labor. Unless the supply can be expanded, an upward pressure on skilled wage rates will result and, to the extent that wage contracts for unskilled laborers are indexed to the development of skilled wages, 'contamination' will result. The overall wage level will thus tend to rise and with it the general price level. In such a situation the Reserve Bank will react by tightening monetary policy. Interest rates, already high,[52] will rise even further, and there will be pressure on the Department of Finance to fall in line so as not to compromise the stabilization effort. The result is that growth, if only temporarily, will be held back. Firms cannot invest and consumer demand falls.

Possibly the growth rate at which the skill constraint may spark off a monetary contraction has been reduced during the last couple of years. South Africa is to an increasing extent experiencing a brain drain of educated whites, who have seen their labor market shrink as affirmative action measures take hold. At the same time, with rising labor costs, there will be a tendency for techniques in manufacturing to become more capital, and hence also skill, intensive.

The tradeoff between stabilization and growth that runs via monetary policy could also come into play as a result of balance of payments trouble. When GDP increases so do imports, and marginal import propensities appear to be high in South Africa. During the recovery from late 1993 to late 1996 the average import penetration ratio (the value of imports in relation to GDP at constant prices) increased from 19 percent to 27 percent. In part this was due to the repeal of trade sanctions and the lowering of tariffs, but there is no doubt that GDP increases tend to result in increased demand for imports as well, via increased real domestic expenditure.[53] To the extent that the increases consist of inputs for the export sectors the pressure on the balance of payments will presumably be tolerable, at least in the somewhat longer run, but non-traded goods require imported inputs as well, and in addition there is a demand for imported consumer goods. Thus growth easily leads to a deficit on the current account of the balance of payments and to a tendency for the rand to depreciate, which makes the Reserve Bank tighten the monetary screw to reduce the threat of imported inflation. Again growth is choked in the process.

In sum, GEAR stands out not so much as a growth strategy but as one for macroeconomic discipline. Unfortunately, the way it is formulated appears to introduce a conflict or tradeoff between growth and stability in the sense that stabilization efforts will get in the way of growth. The government is committed to reducing the budget deficit at a brisk pace and fiscal policy hence has to be contractionary. However, in the best-case scenario, tight monetary policy can be avoided. GEAR envisages a reduction of tariffs that may put competitive pressure on firms and make them refrain from price inflation. However, inflationary pressure may mount from other quarters, not least the labor market. If such be the case, monetary policy will be tightened and the growth rate will be reduced. That puts us back where we started: with investment. Unless domestic and foreign companies react positively in the face of austere policies and turn a blind eye to the lack of growth, the GEAR package will fail to lift the economy.

**The political economy of low growth**

The conclusions from the foregoing should be clear. There is a very real risk that GEAR will fail to deliver the growth necessary for meeting the objectives of the Reconstruction and Development Programme. The crucial elements of the strategy are outside the control of the government and there are strong built-in policy checks on growth. Together these factors will choke the growth process. The South African economy will continue to muddle through, the way it has done since 1993, with some years slightly better than others. Factors like the weather will continue to be decisive for the growth rate, which is likely to remain around 3 percent until the turn of the century.

This is far from enough to enable the delivery of the contents of the RDP. The growth constraint on redistribution and social spending will become stronger, while emphasis on growth will presumably be even more pronounced in the debate, with new (or old) suggestions about how to proceed continuing to enliven it. At the same time, the expansion of formal employment will be sluggish and the disadvantaged among the population will be required to wait or to adjust their expectations downwards.

This message will be delivered in a situation where the gap between the haves and the have-nots among blacks increases rapidly. Between 1975 and 1991 the richest 20 percent of the blacks increased their real income by almost 40 percent. All other black groups saw their position deteriorate, the poorest 40 percent no less than 41.4 percent.[54] This pattern is likely to have been reinforced since 1991. In the post-apartheid economy, the better educated blacks are the ones with the brightest future prospects. Political change and correctness makes it imperative to hire blacks at all levels of the formal labor market. The problem of the poor is that they are not part of this market and the backlog of unemployed is already enormous. Since, on present trends, perhaps only some 5–6 percent of the annual addition to the labor force is absorbed by the formal segment,[55] one can only imagine what sentiments may be building up outside it and the social consequences, including crime, of exclusion.

Pressure is mounting from another quarter as well. After the presentation of the GEAR document, the trade union movement, notably COSATU, has gradually distanced itself from the economic policies of the ANC government. The issues of labor market flexibility and wage restraint have driven a wedge between the traditional allies. COSATU, to an increasing extent, is expressing grassroots sentiments against ANC policy, with the aid of the strike weapon. Not only has it become increasingly vocal with respect to GEAR, but the labor movement as a whole has also reacted against the proposed Basic Conditions of Employment Act, arguing that it provides far fewer employee benefits (in terms of working hours, maternity leave, overtime payment, etc.) than demanded. It is now too late in the day to forge a social accord on the labor market; it should have been done back in 1994 immediately after the elections in the general mood of conciliation that prevailed at the time. Today, with slow growth and little employment creation, the historic moment seems to have passed.

Sooner or later these sentiments will be vented in a different way. Economic and political solutions other than those advocated by the present ANC coalition will be sought. Even though the outcome of the process may not be as dramatic as predicted by Lester Venter (1997), where a new 'African National Labour Party' arises, to the left of the ANC, takes over the government in 2004, and begins to implement a generally populist policy, including the redistribution of a non-growing cake, political pressure may still force the ANC to do something similar. Ultimately, politicians cannot remain isolated from popular sentiment. Economic policy easily moves in cycles[56] and if populism is allowed to carry the day, the consequences sketched in the discussion of distribution-fueled growth will quickly be felt by all South Africans.

## Notes

*Thanks are due to Brian Kahn, Murray Leibbrandt, Lieb Loots, Nicoli Nattrass, Ben Smit and Servaas van der Berg for liberally sharing their views of the problems facing the South African economy with me. An earlier version of the chapter was presented at a seminar at the School of

Oriental and African Studies, University of London, on 1 December 1997. I am grateful to the participants in that seminar, especially Ben Fine, for helpful suggestions.

1    ANC (1994).
2    Lundahl and Moritz (1996), Chapters 9–10.
3    See e.g. Lundahl and Moritz (1994).
4    South African Reserve Bank (1997a), p. 5.
5    Cf. e.g. Horwitz (1967), Botha (1973), Lipton (1985), McCarthy (1988), Fine and Rustomjee (1996).
6    van der Berg and Siebrits (1991), Moll (1991), Standish (1992).
7    Moll (1991), p. 318.
8    Standing, Sender and Weeks (1996), p. 25.
9    Moll (1991), p. 317.
10   Krietzinger-van Niekerk, Eckert and Vink (1992), p. 14.
11   Standish (1992), p. 121.
12   Cf. Dornbusch and Edwards (1990).
13   Notably NIEP (n.d.).
14   ANC (1994).
15   Kahn (1997), p. 2.
16   Lundahl (1997).
17   South African Foundation (1996).
18   Department of Finance (1996a), (1996b).
19   Nattrass (1988), p. 25.
20   Republic of South Africa (1994) p. 21.
21   South African Reserve Bank (1995a).
22   South African Reserve Bank (1995c), p. 7.
23   South African Reserve Bank (1997a), p. 5.
24   Ibid., p. 7.
25   Ibid., p. 6.
26   Standing, Sender and Weeks (1996), p. 25.
27   South African Reserve Bank (1995b), p. 7, (1996), p. 3.
28   South African Reserve Bank (1997a), p. 6.
29   South African Reserve Bank (1995c), p. 8, (1996), pp. 3–4, (1997a), pp. 5–6.
30   South African Reserve Bank (1997a), p. 5.
31   South African Reserve Bank (1995b), pp. 7–8.
32   South African Reserve Bank (1995c), p. 8, (1996), p. 4, (1997a), pp. 6–7.

33    South African Reserve Bank (1996), p. 4.

34    South African Reserve Bank (1997a), p. 5.

35    Nattrass (1988), p. 25.

36    For a criticism of the argument that import substitution behind tariff walls was the main engine of industrial growth in South Africa, see Fine and Rustomjee (1996).

37    Department of Finance (1996b), p. 11.

38    Ibid., pp. 10–11.

39    Ibid., pp. 12–13.

40    Weeks (1996).

41    Gibson and van Seventer (1995).

42    Kahn (1997), p. 2.

43    Nomvete, Maasdorp and Thomas (1997), p. 45.

44    Ibid.

45    Nordås (1996).

46    Department of Finance (1996a), p. 7.

47    Weeks (1996), pp. 10–13.

48    South African Reserve Bank (1997b), p. 1.

49    Department of Finance (1996b), pp. 11, 13.

50    Lachman and Bercuson (1992), p. 29.

51    Lundahl, Moritz and Fredriksson (1992), pp. 312–17.

52    During 1996, the Bank rate was increased from 15 to 17 percent, and the prime overdraft rate of the banks exceeded 20 percent part of the year (Department of Finance (1997), p. 27). Since then, the Bank rate has come down one percentage point.

53    South African Reserve Bank (1997a), p. 23.

54    McGrath and Whiteford (1994), p. 11.

55    van der Berg (1991), p. 22, Standing, Sender and Weeks (1996), p. 109.

56    Krueger (1993).

## References

ANC (African National Congress) (1994), *The Reconstruction and Development Programme.* Umanyano Publications: Johannesburg.

Botha, D.S.S. (1973), 'On Tariff Policy: The Formative Years', *South African Journal of Economics,* Vol. 41.

Department of Finance (1996a), *Growth, Employment and Redistribution: A Macro-Economic Strategy.* Pretoria.

Department of Finance (1996b), *Growth, Employment and Redistribution: A Macro-Economic Strategy (Appendices).* Pretoria.

Department of Finance (1997), *Budget Review 1997.* Pretoria.

Dornbusch, Rudiger and Edwards, Sebastian (1990), 'Macroeconomic Populism', *Journal of Development Economics,* Vol. 32.

Fine, Ben and Rustomjee, Zavareh (1996), *The Political Economy of South Africa: From Minerals-Energy Complex to Industrialisation.* Hurst & Company: London.

Gibson, Bill and van Seventer, Dirk Ernst (1995), *Restructuring Public Sector Expenditure in the South African Economy.* Development Bank of Southern Africa: Halfway House.

Horwitz, Ralph (1967), *The Political Economy of South Africa.* Weidenfeld and Nicolson: London.

Kahn, Brian (1997), Capital Flows and Balance of Payment Crises in South Africa. Revised First Draft. May. School of Economics, University of Cape Town: Cape Town.

Krietzinger-Van Niekerk, Lolette; Eckert, Jerry B. and Vink, Nick (1992), *Toward a Democratic Economy in South Africa: An Approach to Economic Restructuring.* Development Bank of Southern Africa: Halfway House.

Krueger, Anne O. (1993), *Political Economy of Policy Reform in Developing Countries.* MIT Press: Cambridge, MA and London.

Lachman, Desmond and Bercuson, Kenneth, with Daudi Ballalli, Robert Corker, Charalambos Christofides and James Wein (1992), *Economic Policies for a New South Africa,* IMF Occasional Paper No. 91, IMF: Washington, D.C.

Lipton, Merle (1985), *Capitalism and Apartheid. South Africa, 1910-84.* Gower: Aldershot.

Lundahl, Mats (1997), *The South African Economy in 1996: From Reconstruction and Development to Growth, Employment and Redistribution.* SIDA: Stockholm.

Lundahl, Mats; Fredriksson, Per and Moritz, Lena (1992), 'South Africa 1990: Pressure for Change', in Lundahl, Mats, *Apartheid in Theory and Practice: An Economic Analysis.* Westview Press: Boulder, CO.

Lundahl, Mats and Moritz, Lena (1994), 'The Quest for Equity in South Africa – Redistribution and Growth', in Odén, Bertil; Ohlson, Thomas; Davidson, Alex; Strand, Per; Lundahl, Mats and Moritz, Lena, *The South*

*African Tripod: Studies on Economics, Politics and Conflict.* Scandinavian Institute of African Studies: Uppsala.

Lundahl, Mats and Moritz, Lena (1996), *Det nya Sydafrika: Ekonomi och politik efter apartheid.* SNS Förlag: Stockholm.

McCarthy, Colin L. (1988), 'Structural Development of South African Manufacturing Industry', *South African Journal of Economics,* Vol. 56.

McGrath, Michael and Whiteford, Andrew (1994), 'Inequality in the Size Distribution of Income in South Africa', Stellenbosch Economic Project, Occasional Papers, No. 10, Centre for Contextual Hermeneutics, University of Stellenbosch: Stellenbosch.

Moll, Terence (1991), 'Growth through Redistribution: A Dangerous Fantasy?', *South African Journal of Economics,* Vol. 59.

Nattrass, Jill (1988), *The South African Economy: Its Growth and Change.* Second edition. Oxford University Press: Cape Town.

NIEP (National Institute for Economic Policy) (n.d.), *From the RPP to GEAR: The Gradual Embrace of Neo-Liberalism in Economic Policy.* NIEP: Johannesburg.

Nomvete, Bax D; Maasdorp, Gavin G. and Thomas, David (eds.) (1997), *Growth with Equity.* Africa Institute for Policy Analysis and Economic Integration: Cape Town.

Nordås, Hildegunn Kyvik (1996), 'South African Manufacturing Industries – Catching Up or Falling Behind?, *Journal of Development Studies,* Vol. 32.

Republic of South Africa (1994), *South African Statistics.* Central Statistical Service: Pretoria.

*Restructuring the South African Labour Market* (1996*).* Report of the Commission to Investigate the Development of a Comprehensive Labour Market Policy. CTP Book Printers: Cape Town.

*Social Equity and Job Creation: The Key to a Stable Future. Proposals by the South African Labour Movement* (1996). Issued by the Labour Caucus at Nedlac incorporating Cosatu, Nactu and Fedsal. No place given.

South African Foundation (1996), *Growth for All: An Economic Strategy for South Africa.* Johannesburg.

South African Reserve Bank (1995a), *Quarterly Bulletin,* No. 195, March.

South African Reserve Bank (1995b), *Quarterly Bulletin,* No. 197, September.

South African Reserve Bank (1995c), *Annual Economic Report 1995.* Pretoria.

South African Reserve Bank (1996), *Quarterly Bulletin,* No. 199, March.

South African Reserve Bank (1997a), *Annual Economic Report 1997.* Pretoria.

South African Reserve Bank (1997b), *Quarterly Bulletin,* No. 205, September.

Standing, Guy; Sender, John and Weeks, John (1996), *Restructuring the Labour Market: The South African Challenge.* International Labour Office: Geneva.

Standish, Barry (1992), 'Resource Endowments, Constraints and Growth Policies', in Abedian, Iraj and Standish, Barry (eds.), *Economic Growth in South Africa: Selected Policy Issues.* Oxford University Press: Cape Town.

van der Berg, Servaas (1991), 'Prospects for Redistribution of Primary and Secondary Incomes in the Transition to Democracy', unpublished paper for the Conference of the Economic Society of South Africa. Stellenbosch, 2-3 October.

van der Berg, Servaas and Siebrits, Krige (1991) 'Redistribution and Growth', paper presented to a workshop of the Economic Trends Group, Cape Town, 22-24 November.

Venter, Lester (1997), *When Mandela Goes: The Coming of South Africa's Second Revolution.* Doubleday: London.

Weeks, John (1996), *Macroeconomic Strategy: Implications for the North West Province.* School of Oriental and African Studies, University of London: London.

# Index

African Nationalist Congress
(ANC), 9-11, 14-16, 26, 34,
37, 45, 52-53, 58, 65, 73-75,
112, 123-125, 130, 141
Africans, 3, 6, 20-21, 32, 46, 48-
49, 51, 81, 110, 123, 140
- land alienation from, 2-3
Afrikaner capitalists, 5
Afrikaner Weerstandsbeweging,
(AWB), 11
agriculture, 2, 5,19, 48-49, 75-78,
131-132
ANC, see African National
Congress
anti-trust legislation, 55, 100
apartheid, 3, 6, 14-15, 19ff, 32-33,
39, 46-49, 51, 63-65, 87, 93,
138, 140
ARMSCOR, 48, 50
Asians, 20-21, 32, 51, 81, 123
Atlantis Diesel, 50
AWB, see Afrikaner
Weerstandsbeweging

balance of payments, 24-25, 31,
37, 53, 61, 85, 87-91, 107, 127,
136, 139

Bantu Education Act, 46, 51
bantustans, see homelands
basic needs, 53-54, 95
Bhorat, Haroon, 110
Biko, Steve, 4
Bisho, 10
Boer War, 3, 46
Boipatong, 10
Botha, P.W., 1, 5-6
brain drain, 139
Bunting, Brian, 46
Business South Africa, 101
Buthelezi, Mangosuthu, 4, 9, 125

capacity utilization, 23, 25, 37
capital flows, 24, 32, 35, 78, 88,
90, 104, 108, 112, 130, 137
Ciskei, 10
civilized labor policy, 3
CODESA, see Convention for
Democratic South Africa
Coloreds, 20-21, 32, 51, 81, 123
COMESA, see Common Market
of Eastern and Southern Africa
Common Market of Eastern and
Southern Africa (COMESA),
87

Communist Party, 7, 11
comparative advantage, 60, 105-107, 136
Congress of South African Trade Unions (COSATU), 10, 36, 52, 129, 141
Conservative Party, 6-7, 10
constitution, 73
construction, 37, 79, 131
Convention for Democratic South Africa (CODESA), 9-10
COSATU, see Congress of South African Trade Unions

de Klerk, Frederik Willem, 1, 7-11, 46, 123
Declaration of Intent, 10
defense spending, 22
Democratic Party, 7
Democratization Pact, 11
Department of Finance, 36, 56, 61, 74, 98, 112, 139
Development Bank of Southern Africa, 126
diamonds, 78
discouraged workers, 80

economies of scale, 106
education, 22, 26, 32, 34, 39, 51-54, 56, 94, 97, 136, 138
efficiency, 46, 62
electrification, 97
employment, 15, 34, 37-39, 46-47, 54-58, 61-63, 73, 76-77, 79-82, 93, 95, 99, 101-102, 108-111, 134, 140
equality, 51, 56
ESCOM, 97
exchange rate policy, 57, 59, 83, 87-88, 102, 104, 130, 134

export promotion, 50, 60-61
exports, 25, 27, 38-39, 49, 57-61, 88-89, 104, 107, 112, 128, 133-134

financial liberalization, 87, 99
financial services, 79
fiscal policy, 26, 57, 59, 62, 102, 129, 137-139
foreign aid, 95
foreign debt, 87, 90
FOSCOR, 48
Freedom Charter, 15, 46, 52, 93

GATT, see General Agreement on Tariffs and Trade
GEAR, see Growth, Employment and Redistribution
GEIS, see General Export Incentive Scheme
General Agreement on Tariffs and Trade (GATT), 38, 59-60, 95
General Export Incentive Scheme, (GEIS), 85-86, 104, 136
Generalized System of Preferences, 86
gold, 23, 25, 38, 49, 57, 59, 76, 78, 88, 112, 131-133
government budget, 22, 26, 56-58, 62, 83, 91-92, 99-100, 103, 132, 137-138
government expenditure, 22, 32-33, 54, 58, 62, 92, 99-100, 138
Government of National Unity, 1, 8, 10, 16, 33-34, 73-75, 91, 112, 123-124, 128
government revenue, 92
Group Areas Act, 46

growth, 14-16, 19, 21, 23-25, 31, 32, 34-38, 40, 54, 56-59, 61-62, 65, 73, 75, 77, 79, 98, 101-102, 107-108, 111, 124, 126ff, 138-140
- through redistribution, 37
*Growth, Employment and Redistribution* (GEAR), 15, 16, 46, 57, 61-62, 75, 101-103, 107, 112, 130, 132ff, 140-141
*Growth for All*, 57, 99-101, 129

Hani, Chris, 11
health, 21-22, 26, 32, 53-54, 56, 94, 96
Holden, Merle, 50
homelands, 4, 47, 51
housing, 21-22, 32, 37, 51, 54-55, 93, 97
human capital, 105-106, 136, 138
Huntington, Samuel, 73-74

ILO, see International Labour Organization
import substitution, 20, 31, 38, 48, 50-51, 126
imports, 25, 49-51, 88, 139
- liberalization of, 25, 54
income distribution, 20-22, 25, 31-32, 34, 37, 51, 53, 55-56, 58, 62, 73, 79, 82, 93, 101, 110, 124, 128, 140
industrial democracy, 56
industrial policy, 26-27, 34, 49, 95
industry, 3, 31, 37-38, 50, 60, 78, 89, 95, 105, 111, 126, 131-132
inflation, 23, 37, 54, 61, 82-83, 91, 104, 139
influx control of labor, 49
infrastructure, 39, 54, 56, 59, 95, 98

Inkatha, 4, 7-10, 16, 73-74, 123, 125
Inkathagate, 9
interest rates, 24, 132, 134, 139
International Labour Organization (ILO), 64, 80-81, 109
investment, 27, 29, 31, 32, 39-40, 54-55, 58-59, 76, 88, 98, 102-104, 130, 134-137, 140
Iran, 4
ISCOR, 48, 50
Iyengar, Murali, 48

kickstart of the economy, 23, 126-128
KwaZulu, 4

Labour Relations Act, 13
Leibbrandt, Murray, 110

macroeconomic populism, 127
Macroeconomic Research Group (MERG), 26-28, 53
Mandela, Nelson, 7, 9, 36, 52-53, 96, 123, 125
Manuel, Trevor, 98
manufacturing, see industry
Marrakesh Agreement, 85, 104, 132
Mbeki, Thabo, 98, 125
McCarthy, Colin, 86
MERG, see Macroeconomic Research Group
minerals, 39, 46, 104
mining, 2-3, 20, 49, 75-76, 78, 89, 131-132
monetary policy, 23, 37, 57-58, 60-61, 82-84, 91,102-103, 134, 137-139
Mossgas, 50

MPNP, see Multiparty
  Negotiating Process
Multiparty Negotiating Process
  (MPNP), 11

Naidoo, Jay, 97
National African Federated
  Chamber of Commerce and
  Industry, 101
National Economic, Development
  and Labour Council
  (NEDLAC), 12-14
National Economic Forum (NEC),
  13
National Party, 1, 3, 7, 9, 16, 46-
  47, 52, 73-74, 123-125
Nationalist, 8, 10
Nationalist government, 46, 51
National Peace Accord, 8-9
nationalization, 53
Native Trust and Land Act, 48
Natives Land Act, 48
Nattrass, Nicoli, 100
NEC, see National Economic
  Forum
NEDLAC, see National
  Economic, Development
  and Labour Council
Nordås, Hildegunn Kyvik, 105
nutrition, 32, 51, 94

PAC, see Pan-Africanist Congress
Pact Government, 3
Pan-Africanist Congress (PAC), 4

parliamentary elections
  - 1948, 1, 46
  - 1981, 6-7
  - 1992 by-election, 10
  - 1994, 73, 141
  - 1999, 123, 125

Population Registration Act, 46
Porter, Richard, 48
Posel, Deborah, 46
poverty, 51, 55, 62, 64, 79, 82,
  110-111, 140
Preferential Trade Area for
  Eastern and Southern African
  States, 87
Prisoners' Dilemma, 8, 13, 63,
  109
private investment, 28, 34, 40, 53,
  57, 59, 77, 102, 137
PTA, see Preferential Trade Area
  for Eastern and Southern
  African States
public debt, 22-24, 33, 92
public investment, 40, 53, 59
public works, 55

quantitative import restrictions,
  48, 60, 85, 104

racial discrimination, see
  apartheid
raw materials, 27, 38
RDP, see Reconstruction and
  Development Programme
Reconstruction and Development
  Programme (RDP), 14-16, 26,
  34, 37, 39-40, 46, 53-56, 65,
  75, 77, 91, 93-98, 112, 124-
  125, 128, 131, 133, 140
redistribution, 14-15, 37
redistribution through growth, 38
Regional Industrial Development
  Programme, 48
Reservation of Separate
  Amenities Act, 47
Rhodesia, 4
'Rubicon' speech of F.W. de
  Klerk, 7-8

SACU see Southern African Customs Union
SADC, see Southern African Development Community
SALDRU, see South African Labour and Development Research Unit
sanctions against South Africa, 4
SASOL, 48, 50
savings, 25
Schrire, Robert, 74
services, 79
Sharpeville, 4
Sisk, Timothy, 8
Slovo, Joe, 11
Smuts, Jan, 3
social accord, 63-64, 108-109, 135
Social Equity and Job Creation, 100, 129
South African Chamber of Business, 135
South African Foundation, 15, 55-56, 99-101, 129-130, 135
South African Labour and Development Research Unit (SALDRU), 80-81
South African Reserve Bank, 23, 25, 35-36, 58, 61, 82, 84, 88, 91, 138-139
Southern African Customs Union (SACU), 86
Southern African Development Community (SADC), 86
Soweto, 4, 31
stabilization, 23ff, 39, 61, 83, 107, 129, 139
stagflation, 35

stagnation, 31, 128
Stals, Chris, 35, 88

tariffs, 38-39, 48-50, 59-60, 83, 85-86,104, 128, 132, 139
taxes, 21-22, 26, 28, 32-33, 49, 54-55, 57, 60, 62, 76, 92, 99, 130, 135-138
telecommunications, 94
trade policy, 26-27, 34, 38, 49, 87, 95
trade unions, 33, 56, 62-63, 103, 108, 135
transplacement, 73
Treurnicht, Andries, 6

unemployment, 25, 56
- definition of, 80
Unlawful Organizations Act, 4
Uruguay Round, 85

van den Berghe, Pierre, 46
van der Berg, Servaas, 48
Venter, Lester, 141
*verkramptes*, 6
*verligtes*, 6
Verwoerd, Hendrik, 4, 74
Vorster, John, 6

wages, 23, 36, 38-39, 49, 56, 61, 63-64, 79, 82-84, 100-101, 103, 107-111, 129, 132-133, 135, 139
Witwatersrand, 3
World Trade Organization (WTO), 59, 85, 104-105, 136
WTO, see World Trade Organization

Printed and bound by CPI Group (UK) Ltd, Croydon, CR0 4YY
08/05/2025
01864419-0001